HARVARD HISTORICAL MONOGRAPHS
IV

PUBLISHED UNDER THE DIRECTION OF THE DEPARTMENT
OF HISTORY FROM THE INCOME OF

THE ROBERT LOUIS STROOCK FUND

LONDON : HUMPHREY MILFORD

OXFORD UNIVERSITY PRESS

Russian Diplomacy
and the
Opening of the Eastern
Question in 1838 and 1839

BY

PHILIP E. MOSELY

Cambridge

HARVARD UNIVERSITY PRESS

MCMXXXIV

CONTENTS

26266

PREFACE

In completing this study I wish to express my appreciation of the constant guidance and advice given me by Professor William L. Langer, of Harvard University. Professor Sidney B. Fay likewise assisted me with his advice and encouragement. Professor M. M. Karpovich gave me freely the benefit of his erudition in Russian and Asiatic history. My sincere thanks are due to Harvard University and to its Department of History in particular for the year's grant of the Archibald Cary Coolidge Fellowship, which enabled me to visit Russia in the course of my research.

The Central Archive Administration of the R.S.F.S.R. made this work possible by admitting me to work freely in the diplomatic materials of the period 1838-1842. I wish to express my appreciation of its liberality. The technical assistants of the Archive of Foreign Policy deserve the expression of my thanks for their ever-willing cooperation.

P. E. M.

Schenectady, New York
January 30, 1934

RUSSIAN DIPLOMACY AND THE
OPENING OF THE EASTERN QUESTION
IN 1838 AND 1839

I

Russian Foreign Policy and the Eastern Question

The position of Russia in Europe and Asia was most imposing during the reigns of Alexander I and Nicolas I. By 1815 their empire had reached the farthest western limit of its expansion. It maintained the largest standing army in Europe. Its economic policy was directed towards securing a high degree of industrial self-sufficiency, while making the most of its geographical advantages in Asiatic markets. Russia's policy in Europe was conservative. After 1830 it aimed at maintaining the *status quo* in Central Europe. Nicolas I looked with like suspicion upon the capitalist development of Germany under the Zollverein and on the liberal and national strivings of German, Austrian, Italian, Hungarian, and Polish revolutionaries. Nicolas regarded his empire as an island of order and calm amid a sea of revolutionary passions and dangers, and at crucial moments he had to weigh his eastern policies against Russia's mission of upholding the conservative cause in Europe. The disunion between Russia's policies in Europe and in Asia, which even Nicolas I was unable at all times to harmonize, remained typical of Imperial Russia to its very end.

In the 1830's Russian policy was active in Persia and Afghanistan. After 1833 Russian influence had been predominant at Teheran, and Count Simonich had not discouraged Shah Mohamed from his ambition of conquering Herat, the key to northwest Afghanistan. In 1837 Petersburg and Kabul had for the first time entered into direct relations, and in 1838 that new influence was employed to form a Perso-Afghan alliance, which, under Russian guidance, should dominate the Middle East, open new outlets to Russian commerce, and set a barrier to the expansive tendency of British India. These were large commitments, and contracted at a great distance from the metropolis by agents who could have but an imperfect idea of their repercussions on other fields of Russian diplomatic activity. In 1838 England relieved this sudden pressure on her Afghan flank by a fresh threat to Russia's position in the Near East. The manœuvre succeeded. Russia, in October 1838, relaxed her pressure on the Middle East, in order to defend even more essential interests in Turkey.

Russia's policy in Turkey was dictated by the economic and military necessity for dominating the Straits of Constantinople. The annexation of the northern shores of the Black Sea towards the close of the eighteenth century had been followed by the rapid growth of Russian population, agriculture and commerce in those fertile provinces. Since 1801 Russia had been expanding her power over the eastern end of the Black Sea, but the successful conclusion of her long and bitter struggle with the mountaineers of the Caucasus demanded that Russia's control of that sea should not be challenged by any great Power. After the treaty of Adrianople the Danubian Principalities had come under Russian protectorate, and even though they had been evacuated, Russia continued to exercise close supervision over their internal affairs and still possessed the mouths of the Danube. One school of Russian expansionists, headed by Count Kiselev, the reorganizer of Moldavia and Vallachia, urged that Russia maintain her direct control over these Principalities, as an essential stepping-stone to Constantinople itself. The main current of Russian foreign policy under Nicolas I preferred, however, to use neither the eastern nor the western land-bridge between Russia and the Bosphorus. It believed that Russia was strong enough to control the Straits in one of two other ways. Either Turkey would remain, as under the treaty of Unkiar Iskelessi, the dependent of Russia, thus securing to her northern ally practical domination of that essential water-way. If, on the other hand, Turkey became hostile, or if the Ottoman Empire broke up,—and these two cases seemed synonymous in the 1830's,—Russia would seize the Straits, to keep them forever. And there was one factor in the Levant which compelled Sultan Mahmud to cling to his dangerous protector and obliged Europe to expect in the immediate future the break-up of his exhausted and distracted state. That was the rise of the power of Mohamed Ali in Egypt.

For many years the Pasha of Egypt had built up his rule without attracting the attention of Europe. When he emerged into the public eye, it was in a brilliant role. He was a Europeanizer, the only Mohammedan ruler who knew how to adapt western technique to the social and political conditions of the Levant. His engineering projects, his factories, his masterly manipulation of the resources of Egypt, his

fleet, the religious toleration maintained within his
territories, finally his ambition to become an independent ruler drew to him the attention of military
adventurers, machinery salesmen, tourists, Saint-
Simonians. In 1833 the question of the future relation of Mohamed Ali to the Ottoman Empire had been
brought to a head by the swift conquest of Syria, and
his threat to Constantinople. Russia's intervention
to protect the Sultan in his capital had established
her paramount influence over the Porte, and compelled
England and France to mediate a compromise, more
expedient than satisfactory, between the Sultan and
his vassal. The convention of Kutaya had irked both
its signatories, and not a year passed after 1833 without an attempt by one or both to throw its terms into
the discard. But between 1833 and 1838 the situation
had shifted, and not to the benefit of the Pasha's
ambition. England, alarmed at the danger that the
Straits might pass into Russia's direct possession, was
directly injured by the growing power of Mohamed
Ali, whose new state straddled the two chief routes
between Great Britain and India. It was certain in
1838 that England would not be, as in 1833, an idle
spectator of what might occur in the Levant. When
Mohamed Ali announced, on May 25, 1838, his determination to make himself independent of the Sultan, two European interests were immediately thrown
into play: the future of Egypt and the future of the
Straits.

II

RUSSIA AND THE STRAITS

IN the 1830's Russian policy with respect to the Straits
of the Dardanelles and Bosphorus was characterized
by a mingled feeling of hope and fear. There was a
hope that her Black Sea fleet, stationed only four
days' sail from the Bosphorus, would be able, at some
moment of confusion in Constantinople and of disunion among the Powers, to seize the Straits. There
was fear, sometimes inclining to deadly certainty, that
this bold stroke would lead to a war against the rest
of Europe. And mingled with that hope and fear was
a fatalistic conception, recurring again and again in
the mind of Nicolas I himself, that the inevitable fall
of the Sultan's government would force Russia to this
step, if only to protect herself against the seizure of
the "keys to her house" by England and France,
or by either one of them.

The moment at which Russia could have seized
the Straits—though with little chance of holding them
against a European coalition—occurred in September 1829. The Russian army had its headquarters
at Adrianople and Russian guns could be heard in
Constantinople. To the Tsarist ambassador in Paris,
Count Pozzo di Borgo, it seemed as if the fruit were
ready to fall into the outstretched hand. This skillful diplomat, the compatriot and deadly foe of that
other and greater Corsican, possessed the same vivid

imagination, the same readiness for visualizing a
hundred possible situations; and his advice was usually
martial, although he never had to carry into effect the
military combinations which he brought forth with
such an easy touch. At the very time that the Russian commander in Rumelia, Diebitsch, was drawing
up the terms of peace, Pozzo di Borgo, from Paris,
sketched the "Russian solution" of the Eastern question, as he saw it. Russia should occupy the Bosphorus and Dardanelles, thus assuring for herself
absolute control of the route from the Black Sea to
the Mediterranean. Constantinople should be a free
port. The disposition of the emancipated provinces of
European Turkey could be left to a conference of the
Powers, to be summoned by Russia, clothed in her
new prestige.[1]

But at this moment a less aggressive view prevailed.
The Russian army had spent its force in advancing
up to the very Straits. It had to think of its depleted
ranks, of the financial havoc wrought by a war which
had proved longer and more difficult than expected.
And in Transylvania Austria was waiting. On the
sea the English were on the watch. In Constantinople
itself the ambassador of Russia's sole and half-hearted
ally, France, was intriguing to stop the Russian advance. This was no time to defy Europe, to provoke
Austria and France to join the British. The policy
adopted in the Treaty of Adrianople, and maintained
throughout the 1830's, was that the Ottoman Empire
must be preserved against premature dissolution until

[1] F. F. Martens, "Rossia i Frantsia vo vremena restavratsii i
iyul'skoi monarkhii," *Zhurn. Min. Narod. Prosv.*, 1907, X, 240-241.

more favorable circumstances should permit Russia to take the share appropriate to her as the most powerful neighbor. The corollary to this general proposition was that friendship should be maintained with Turkey, since it was preferable that the Straits be in the hands of a weak and officially amicable government rather than in those of any European state. The policy of supporting the Porte against external menace found its most vivid expression in the Russian expedition of 1833 to defend Constantinople and Mahmud against the advance of the Egyptians under Ibrahim Pasha. Fearful that a more powerful and more Europeanized régime might be established in the Ottoman Empire if the Sultan and his un-vassal-like Pasha were allowed to finish their duel without interference, the Russian government took a momentous decision. It provoked an appeal of the Sultan and answered that appeal by sending a squadron and landing-force to the Bosphorus. The reward which Russia exacted before withdrawing her troops was the treaty of alliance of July, 1833.

Russia's interest in the Straits was stated in concrete form by the treaty of Unkiar Iskelessi, signed on July 8, 1833, between Russia and the Ottoman Porte. That treaty has represented to some historians the farthest advance ever made by Russia towards solving the problem of the Straits in her own favor and to the exclusion of other influences. To contemporary Russian statesmen, however, that treaty seemed only a half-way mark on the road to "Tsargrad," not the goal itself. The confusion aroused by the 1833 treaty was the basis of conflicting views stated in the following years by the various governments and the cause of several misunderstandings which have persisted till the present day.

Some writers have directed their attention towards the question of the Straits alone. Their status was alleged to be determined by a separate and secret article, appended to the treaty of alliance: "The Sublime Ottoman Porte, in place of the assistance which it must lend in case of need, in accordance with the principle of reciprocity of the open Treaty, shall limit its action in favor of the Imperial Court of Russia to closing the Straits of the Dardanelles, that is, to not allowing any foreign vessel of war to enter them under any pretext whatsoever." What was the significance of this stipulation?

At this time the status of the Straits was determined by the Anglo-Turk Treaty of 1809. Article XI of that treaty reads as follows: "Since it has been in all times forbidden for war vessels to enter the channel of Constantinople; that is, the Strait of the Dardanelles and that of the Black Sea, and since this ancient rule of the Ottoman Empire ought likewise to be observed henceforward in time of peace towards every Power whatsoever, the British Court also promises to conform to this principle." Did the secret article of 1833 change this situation?

In the mind of Nesselrode, it did not change the situation as far as the Porte was concerned. "At bottom this stipulation will not impose any new burden on the Porte, for, in any case, it is interested, by its own security, in keeping the entrance of the Dardanelles closed to foreign vessels of war, and the prin-

ciple is fixed in fact and consecrated by the usage of
all time. It will, therefore, by no means be an onerous
obligation for the Porte to state and confirm, by an
express stipulation, the existence of a principle to
which it has invariably held." [2] To Nesselrode, then,
in drawing up the instructions for concluding the
treaty of 1833, the secret article on the Straits did
not contain any provisions contradictory to the principle, maintained by the Porte, of closing the Straits
to all warships. Nesselrode repeated this point of
view in his despatch of August 5/17, 1833, which was
intended to explain to the Powers the conclusion of
the treaty. The secret article "does not impose on
the Porte any burdensome condition and does not cause
it to contract any new engagement. It serves only to
state the fact of the closure of the Dardanelles for the
military flag of the foreign Powers; a system which
the Porte has maintained at all times and from which,
indeed, it could not depart without injuring its most
direct interests." [3]

But this interpretation of the secret article was not
accepted by many contemporaries. Guizot thus sum-
marized the situation which had been created: "Thus
the Cabinet of St. Petersburg, converting into a written law the fact of its preponderance at Constantinople,
made Turkey into its official client and the Black Sea
into a Russian lake, the entrance of which was guarded

---

[2] Nesselrode to Orlov, instructions for concluding an alliance with
the Porte, May 8, 1833, o.s., in S. M. Goriainov, *Le Bosphore et les
Dardanelles*, Paris, 1910, p. 40.

[3] F. F. Martens, *Recueil des traités et conventions conclus par la
Russie avec les Puissances étrangères*, 15 vols., St. Petersburg, 1874-
1909, in XII, 43-44.

by this client against Russia's possible enemies, without anything hindering Russia herself from passing
through it and hurling her ships and her soldiers into
the Mediterranean." [4]   This has also been the usual
English view of the treaty. "It guaranteed to Russia
a free passage for her warships through the Straits
and it closed the door into the Black Sea to every
other Power." [5]   W. Alison Phillips,[6] followed by
Buxton and Phillipson,[7] asserted that the undertak-
ing of the Porte to close the Dardanelles to the warships of all nations "in case of need" meant not only
that the passage of the Straits would be denied to
foreign warships at Russia's demand, but that the
Tsar was entitled to demand the passage for his own
fleet in either direction, between the Mediterranean
and the Black Seas.

This question has been much confused by the reasoning introduced by Goriainov.[8]   ". . . According
to the secret article, the Porte was bound, if the Emperor demanded it, to lend him assistance by closing
the Dardanelles to the British fleet from the Mediterranean side; as for the Russian fleet, according to the
sense of the treaty taken as a whole, it enjoyed the
liberty of passing through the Straits from the Black

[4] F. P. G. Guizot, *Mémoires pour servir à l'histoire de mon temps*,
new ed., Paris, 1872, IV, 49.

[5] J. A. R. Marriott, *The Eastern Question*, 3rd ed., Oxford, 1924,
p. 236.

[6] *Cambridge Modern History*, X, ch. xvii, 555.

[7] Coleman Phillipson and Noel Buxton, *The Question of the Bosphorus and Dardanelles*, London, 1917, p. 66; also C. W. Crawley,
"Anglo-Russian Relations 1815-1840," *Cambridge Historical Journal*,
1929, p. 72.

[8] Goriainov, *op. cit.*, pp. 43-44.

Sea into the Mediterranean to attack the enemy's fleet." Goriainov does not base this far-reaching claim, attributed to the signers of the 1833 treaty, on any documentary evidence, although he had the full run of the archives for that period. He grounds it in *a posteriori* reasoning of his own. According to him, the preface to the 1833 treaty renewed the clause of the 1805 treaty between Russia and the Porte which guaranteed free passage to Russian ships "on all occasions." However, the preface to the 1833 treaty is the usual one, introducing many treaties, and such a preface, if interpreted literally, would mean that many contradictory clauses of earlier treaties were automatically continued in force. It is the clauses of a treaty, not the general preface, which have force in international law. The 1805 treaty had been denounced in 1806 by Turkey, and clause VII of it had never since been appealed to in practice. Why was Goriainov so anxious to make valid this highly captious and, from a juridical point of view, artificial reasoning? It may be guessed that, as a representative of pre-War Russian diplomacy, he desired to justify the historic urge to secure a "Russian" solution of the Straits problem.

This very point as to Russian privileges in the Straits was seized upon by Palmerston in his controversy over the Unkiar Iskelessi treaty. He "tried to demonstrate that in virtue of this article (the secret article) the Dardanelles would henceforth be closed to the flag of all Powers who might be at war with Russia and open only to the Russian fleet of war. The act of Unkiar Iskelessi thus revoked the Anglo-Turk Treaty of

1809, by which England had taken on herself the engagement to respect the closure of the Dardanelles, if they remained closed to the war flag of all nations without exception." In reply to this declaration by the English minister, the Russian ambassador, Lieven, read to him Count Nesselrode's despatch of August 17, 1833, which proved in the most categorical manner that the passage of the Strait was forbidden to all warships without exception, and that the Turco-Russian treaty of alliance thus did not establish any privilege in favor of Russia. Palmerston retorted ironically: "But if this treaty did not bring you any advantages or new privileges, then who urged you to conclude it?" [9]

Russia did receive very great advantages, but not those imagined by contemporary statesmen and by later students of international law. But before treating these we must mention the fact that Russia was not inclined to use her Black Sea fleet in the Mediterranean in the 1830's. Only her interest as one of the three protectors of the new Greek kingdom could induce her, as in 1833 and 1834, to send a fleet to those waters. At no time did the Russian cabinet feel that the Russian fleet could be of any use in settling the Egyptian question proper, and the request made to Russia to join her fleet to those of France and England was regarded by the ministers of Nicolas I as a trick to take the Russian fleet hostage and thus force Russia to subordinate her actions to those of the European concert.[10]

[9] F. F. Martens, *Recueil, etc.,* XII, 50.
[10] See *infra* pp. 75-76.

At the beginning of 1838 a discussion arose among the highest officials of the Russian government as to the rights and privileges of Russia in the Straits. The Emperor Nicolas and the minister of marine, Menshikov, had resolved on sending a squadron of the Baltic fleet around Europe to enter the Dardanelles. Nesselrode was asked, more or less as an afterthought, to arrange for the squadron to take on fresh water and supplies at the ports of Sardinia, since the conservative principles of that kingdom made it the most suitable for this service. For Nicolas I and Menshikov there was evidently no doubt as to Russia's right to enjoy the passage of the Straits. But Nesselrode at once took alarm at this resolution of the Emperor, and drew up a report to prove that it was neither *legal* nor *politic* to send the Russian fleet through the Dardanelles.[11] The guiding principle of the Emperor's eastern policy was to protect his southern provinces by watching over the closure of the Dardanelles. That ancient principle of the Porte had been acknowledged by the Anglo-Turk treaty of 1809. "However, there was no *direct engagement* by which the Porte was bound *towards us* also to maintain the closure of the Dardanelles *in case of war* between Russia and other Powers. It is this gap which our treaty of alliance of the 26 June/8 July, 1833, has served to fill . . . The result is that in the present state of our relations with Turkey, the treaties oblige the latter *to close* the entrance to the Dardanelles to any foreign war flag, but these transactions by no means oblige

[11] See Appendix A.

it *to open* it to us. The treaty of Adrianople, confirmed by that of Constantinople, stipulates explicitly
in our favor only free passage for *merchant* ships; but
no stipulation authorizes us to demand in the Bosphorus the admission of our *war-ships.*" [12] This view,
as expressed by Nesselrode in a confidential report
to the Emperor in January 1838, did not differ, therefore, from his opinion on the same subject expressed
in 1833.

But the political side of the question of the passage
of the Russian fleet through the Straits had still to
be answered. This side of it was developed with great
precision in Nesselrode's report. Turkey would either
refuse or accept the request made by its Russian ally.
It could refuse; it had every legal ground to do so;
and Russia would have nothing to object to its refusal.
But such a refusal would greatly injure Russian prestige and would seriously affect Russia's relations with
her Turkish ally. Or Turkey might grant permission for the Russian fleet to pass the Straits. Then
England and France would at once demand the same
privilege for their own fleets. Russia would have no
grounds for blaming the Porte since it would have

[12] Italics everywhere as in original. In his report Nesselrode
ignored the precedent of 1833. At that time a Russian squadron coming from the Baltic cruised in Greek waters under the command of
Admiral Ricord, and with the permission of the Sultan passed into
the Black Sea. Palmerston promptly declared to the Ottoman
minister in London, Mavrojeni, that since the Russian warships had
had the liberty of passing the Dardanelles, those of England would
have the same right, in accordance with the treaty of 1809 (Goriainov,
op. cit., p. 45). Nesselrode must have felt that, although England
did not carry out that threat in 1833, she would not let such a challenge go unanswered in 1838.

itself broken down the barrier. If Turkey admitted the Russian fleet and kept out the French and English ones, Russia would face the most unfavorable of all wars, one in which she had nothing to gain and great commercial interests to lose. But if the Sultan yielded to the Anglo-French demand, Russia would destroy with her own hands the barrier intended to secure her own safety; she would lose an ally who had been faithful thus far and turn Turkey over to the influence of England and France.

Either a refusal or a concession of the passage of the Straits by the Russian fleet was "so serious that before deciding to run that risk, the interest of Your Majesty's service requires examining seriously the consequences for which we must be prepared; the sacrifices which Russia will have to make; the measures of precaution so that we may be ready, whatever may come, to support the dignity of Russia if it is compromised, to defend its safety if it is in danger."

For Nesselrode, the question of the passage of the Straits by a Russian fleet was not a legal, but a political problem, and as a political problem it meant facing the rest of the world in battle. The question remained as to whether the rest of the world would have Turkey on its side or not. Nesselrode thought that Turkey would escape from Russian influence, and regarded such a war, the alignment of the future Crimean War, as "the most unfavorable of all wars."

For Nesselrode the 1833 treaty did not set up any new régime in regard to the Straits. But its importance lay in the political side of the treaty, in the relationship which it set up between Russia and Turkey. What does the treaty itself say as to that?

"Since this alliance aims only at the common defense of Their States against any encroachment, Their Majesties promise to come to agreement without reserve on all matters concerning their respective tranquillity and safety and, for this purpose, mutually to lend each other material aid and the most effective assistance." [13]   Article 3 explained what the military assistance was to consist in. "In consequence of the principle of mutual preservation and defense which is the basis of the present treaty and because of the most sincere desire to ensure the duration, maintenance and complete independence of the Sublime Porte, His Majesty, the Emperor of All the Russias, in case circumstances arose which might again determine the Sublime Porte to ask for the naval and military assistance of Russia, promises to furnish by land and by sea as many troops and forces as the two high contracting Powers should judge necessary. Accordingly, it is agreed that in this case the land and sea forces, assistance of which the Sublime Porte might claim, are held at its disposition." [14]

[13] "Cette alliance ayant uniquement pour objet la défense commune de Leurs Etats contre tout empiètement, Leurs Majestés promettent de s'entendre sans réserve sur tous les objets qui concernent leur tranquillité et sûreté respectives, et de se prêter à cet effet mutuellement des secours matériels et l'assistance la plus efficace."

[14] "En conséquence du principe de conservation et de défense mutuelle qui sert de base au présent traité et par suite du plus sincère désir d'assurer la durée, le maintien et l'entière indépendance de la Sublime Porte, Sa Majesté l'Empereur de toutes les Russies, dans le cas où les circonstances, qui pourraient déterminer de nouveau la Sublime Porte à réclamer l'assistance navale et militaire de la Russie,

When the Unkiar Iskelessi Treaty was first made, the Russians seem actually to have believed that the Sultan would "come to an understanding without reserve" with the Emperor on any subject affecting the "tranquillity or safety" of Turkey. Nesselrode wrote triumphantly to Lieven in London: [15] ". . . It will henceforth prevent the Porte from drifting, as it has done this time, among England, France and Russia, since it is only the last named which has promised it aid and protection by a formal transaction. . . . Our intervention in the affairs of Turkey has acquired a basis of legality."

Palmerston's first reports from Constantinople led him to declare that Turkey had become Russia's vassal. He based this on the imperfect translation, furnished by the Porte, of the secret article. According to it, "the Porte promised to assist Russia in a war against any European power." [16] This had been proposed, but was rejected by the Russian negotiators in Constantinople, since it was felt, and justly, that it would lead inevitably to a war of Russia and Turkey against a European coalition. But in the Russian interpretation, the treaty was nearly equivalent to establishing a status of vassal for Turkey. The phrase, "s'entendre sans réserve," meant

venaient à se présenter, promet de fournir par terre et par mer autant de troupes et de forces que les deux hautes parties le jugeraient nécessaire. D'après cela, il est convenu qu'en ce cas les forces de terre et de mer, dont la Sublime Porte réclamerait le secours, sont tenues à sa disposition."

15 F. F. Martens, *Recueil, etc.,* XII, 43; Nesselrode to Lieven, London, confidential, July 24, 1833, o.s.

16 F. F. Martens, *Recueil, etc.,* XII, 48.

to them that Turkey could not make any political agreement hostile to Russia, and that in case of complication, the Porte had to consult Russia first and appeal first for Russian aid, if any assistance should be needed. The Porte, and its European friends, naturally strove to attach a less restrictive interpretation to this clause. They maintained that the 1833 treaty assured good understanding between the two parties and military support if Turkey desired it. But they also asserted that Turkey could ask advice wherever she wished, and enter into other pacts without consulting Russia, and even accept the aid of other Powers in preference to that of Russia.

Russia's real aim in making the treaty of 1833 was therefore to secure recognition from the Porte of her paramount interest in Turkey and of her previous right of intervention, to the exclusion of the alliance and intervention of other Powers. This was her real interest in making the treaty, and Nesselrode in his instructions to Orlov set that as the chief aim of the treaty to be concluded. "Lastly, in our own interest, the existence of a treaty of alliance will justify, if circumstances arise, the presence and use of our forces and will permit us again to be on the ground the first and the strongest in the theatre of events, so as always to remain masters of the question, either admitting the preservation of the Ottoman empire as possible, or finally admitting its dissolution as inevitable." [17]

From this it becomes obvious that the chief interest of Russia in making the treaty of Unkiar Iskelessi

[17] Nesselrode to Orlov, May 8, 1833, o.s., Goriainov, *op. cit.*, p. 39.

was not in the immediate advantages it gave, not even in closing the Dardanelles, for its statesmen were quite aware that the secret article merely confirmed towards Russia a general rule which was to the advantage of Turkey itself. Its real interest was in preparing the way for a repetition of the 1833 expedition, and in accustoming the Porte to the position of vassal. Or, if the dissolution of the Ottoman Empire could be pronounced actually accomplished, it entitled Russia to be first on the ground, in order to take what she desired, or at least to make sure that no other Power took it. The alliance, by preparing the ground for Russian intervention, made it possible that Russia might be called upon to aid her ally at any time. A new expedition to Constantinople would probably be the signal for fulfilling Russia's permanent aims in the Straits.

This feeling was general among Russian leaders. Even before the alliance had been drawn up, Orlov wrote to Nesselrode: "There is no doubt but that in a year or two at the most, we shall be summoned back, but we shall have the great advantage of coming back, thanks to our antecedents, without arousing suspicion and of coming back in such a way as never to leave again, if need be." [18] Even Matuscewicz, first secretary in London, wrote in a letter addressed from the hunting festivities of Melton Mowbray in England that "Russia ought always to be ready to take the jump on her enemies by a fleet and an army which

[18] April 25, 1833, o.s., Goriainov, *op. cit.*, p. 35.

can at any time occupy the Straits of the Bosphorus and Dardanelles." [19]

There is evidence, however, that in sending the expedition of 1833 to the shores of the Bosphorus, Nicolas had not intended to withdraw with the more or less innocuous treaty of July 8, 1833. This evidence is not found in Goriainov or in Martens. In October, 1838, at the height of the tension with England over Persian and Afghan affairs, the Russian leaders had to consider how they were to persuade the English to leave Karak and thus to relax the pressure put upon the Shah's government. If friendly persuasion and admonition failed, Russia would occupy some advantageous point on Persia's Caspian shore and remain there until the English withdrew from Karak in the Persian Gulf. In a footnote to a confidential report of Nesselrode to the Emperor, there is the following statement: [20] "It is well understood that this provisional occupation, so far from appearing to be an act of hostility against Persia, will be accompanied by all necessary consideration for the Shah's authority and will be carried out in exactly the same manner in which the Emperor had planned the occupation of a fortified point on the Bosphorus during the events of 1833 in Turkey." From this it is clear that Nicolas had expected that his troops on the Bosphorus would not merely encamp at Unkiar

---

[19] Matuscewicz to Nesselrode, December 2, 1833, o.s., in F. F. Martens, *Recueil, etc.*, XII, 46.

[20] Russian Archives (hereafter referred to as R. A.), folio 66, *Rapports à l'Empereur*, 1838. "Rapport sur les affaires de la Perse," le 15 Octobre, o.s., pp. 188-240.

Iskelessi, but would fortify some point controlling the Straits of the Bosphorus. Was this his original intention, abandoned only in the face of European opposition? Was it to be carried out only in case the Egyptians continued their advance to the walls of Constantinople? Was it to be performed only if the French or English fleets forced the Dardanelles and entered the Golden Horn? These suppositions must be left without answer; but this passage makes it plain that not all the Russian intentions in 1833 have been cleared up even now. If Nicolas had projected the permanent occupation of a fortified point, his agents, in any case, went prepared to accept a treaty of alliance with Turkey as a second best alternative, as a temporary postponement of Russia's eventual possession of the Straits.

The treaty of 1833 offered only a potential advantage to Russia. In case of a possible dissolution of the Turkish Empire, Russia would have the right to interfere as friend. This was all the more important since the natural strategical advantages of Russia were not great enough to ensure success. Russia needed to be sure of a political advantage over England and France in Constantinople in order to make certain that she would not be deprived of her share of booty at the decisive moment. The Turkish government was unable to defend itself; it could not defend the Straits against the French and English fleets, which could go from their usual cruising base at Smyrna and bombard Odessa and Sevastopol before their presence in the Black Sea would become known in St. Petersburg. Russian intervention, to be effective, had to forestall their passing the Straits. But that was possible only by Russia's intervention under guise of friendly assistance to the Porte.

This project never left the mind of the Emperor Nicolas, or those of his advisors, throughout the eastern crisis. But the one danger of the project was that it might call forth a European coalition against Russia. It was English indifference in 1833 that had made it possible for Russia to interfere alone. But after the conclusion of the treaty of Unkiar Iskelessi, English unconcern gave way to vigilance, and Russian policy was closely watched from then on. Russia had no fear of either England or France alone, but their united forces would confront Russia with what Nesselrode called "the most unfavorable of all wars."

The possible attitude of Austria presented another ominous enigma. In European policy Metternich was anxious to maintain the united front of the three Eastern monarchies, Russia, Prussia and Austria. This was essential if the national and liberal movements in Central and Southern Europe were to be contained by the forces of the Austrian monarchy. Vienna's attention was directed towards Italy, where the French government still maintained its occupation of Ancona. That occupation had early lost whatever revolutionizing significance it had originally possessed, but it remained as a symbol to Austria that her guardianship over the Italian states was not unchallenged. And while Metternich and Nicolas worked harmoniously in supporting the conservative interest in European affairs, their material interests differed in the Eastern Question. Despite Pozzo di Borgo's hope that Austria would be willing to cooperate in the liquidation of that question and to make "a few useful acquisitions for herself," there was little hope that Metternich could be brought to change his policy at a time when Austria's military and financial power were in decay, and when her full attention had to be given to the German Confederation and the Italian states.

In 1833 Metternich declared to the French Ambassador in Vienna, "It would be better for the Empire of Austria to face the risk of a war of extermination rather than to see Russia aggrandized by a single village at the expense of the Turkish Empire." [21]

This rhetorical emphasis failed to convince Paris or London that Metternich would actually endanger his European position by going against Russia in the Straits question. "If the Austrian government were reduced to the alternative of breaking with Russia, or of letting her do whatever she wanted to, up to and including the occupation of Constantinople, it is plain to me, at least, that she would resign herself to that," the French prime minister wrote to his ambassador, in reply to these under-cover assurances of Metternich. [22]

During the Russian expedition to the Straits in 1833 Metternich loudly proclaimed his confidence that Russia would withdraw, as Nicolas had promised *urbi et orbi*. Under this guarantee of Russia's honesty of intention there was hidden a threat which Austria

[21] Comte de Ste. Aulaire, *Souvenirs,* Paris, 1926, p. 60.
[22] *Ibid.,* p. 63.

might apply if the need came. In the long run, Russia could not remain in Constantinople without establishing land communications through the Danubian Principalities and Bulgaria. In 1833 those communications were still maintained through the occupation of the Turkish fortress of Silistria, on the right bank of the Danube; and in 1838 Russia had an army corps under Gerstenzweig ready to reoccupy the Principalities in case the landing force at Constantinople should require the throwing out of these long and tenuous lines of communication. By mobilizing in Transylvania, Austria could threaten to break this line and force the Russians to recoil to the Pruth. Military necessity therefore forced the Russian government to abandon its attempt to carry on a completely independent policy in regard to Turkey. No sooner had Russia signed the Unkiar Iskelessi Treaty with Turkey than she began to prepare the ground for a new agreement with Austria. This agreement, signed in the autumn of 1833 at Münchengrätz, greatly limited Russian freedom of action in the Eastern Question. By it Russia bound herself not to undertake action in the Eastern Question without consulting Austria. In case of danger of dissolution of the Turkish Empire, Russia and Austria would act in concert.

Austria tried, from 1833 to 1838, to enlarge the scope of the Münchengrätz agreement. Since it was by no means aggressive in form, nor in Metternich's intention, he saw no objection to inviting England and France to join it. This proposal Nicolas always rejected. It was one thing to have to consult Austria, his client and neighbor; it was quite another to give to the two Western Powers a lever through which to control his own eastern policy. And even Metternich's cautious approaches to Paris and London on this question met with no sympathy because he invariably began his despatches on this question with stilted praise of Russian policy, not at all to the taste of the French or English.[23]

Major Hall has put forth the conception that Russia radically changed her policy towards Turkey between the treaty of July 1833 and the Münchengrätz agreement of the autumn of the same year. It was only pride which prevented Nicolas from enlarging that pact to include England. "Sincerely desirous as he was to conciliate the English government, he would not consent to admit, so long as France and Great Britain were intimately united, that Russia had renounced her old ambition of establishing her power upon the Bosphorus." [24] It is difficult to see on what grounds it could be assumed that Russia had made an about-face in her Straits policy. Certainly, in 1838 there was no doubt in the minds of Nicolas and his advisers that under definite circumstances, Russia must and would occupy the Straits, this time to stay. It was for this purpose that Russia had acquired in the Unkiar Iskelessi Treaty a presumptive right of intervention in Turkey.

But as order came gradually to be restored in the Near East, the possibility for Russia to use her newly-

[23] *Ibid.,* p. 236.
[24] Major John Hall, *England and the Orleans Monarchy,* London, 1912, p. 168.

acquired right of intervention receded. Both Russia and England were willing to postpone the trial of strength. That was especially felt when Palmerston was succeeded by Wellington. The English premier proposed to Russia that she abandon the advanced position which she had adopted in Constantinople. "After that experiment, after the Court of Russia is convinced and proves to us that this treaty is at bottom of no real importance for her, why, if the Sultan lent himself to it on his side, should she not renounce a pact which arouses against her, to such a high degree, national animosity in all countries and chiefly in this country?" [25]   This offer had already been met half-way by Nesselrode's letter: ". . . so long as a state of peace, in such agreement with our wishes, continues, this treaty will rest in our archives, as an historic document of which Russia is proud, but whose effects she is by no means anxious to invoke." [26]   Beneath this apparent readiness to leave the treaty in abeyance was a determination to use it for Russia's advantage in case peace could not be prolonged, for every proposition has its converse.

After 1833 the struggle between Russia and the two Western Powers was expressed in an effort to manœuvre each other into an unfavorable position. Russia's aim was to manœuvre France and England into a position where they could no longer oppose a united and probably successful resistance to her ambitions regarding Constantinople. She wanted at the

[25] Medem to Nesselrode, 22 January/3 February, 1835, F. F. Martens, *Recueil, etc.*, XII, 56-57.

[26] Nesselrode to Pozzo, January 14, 1835, o.s., *ibid.*, XII, 58.

same time to keep Austria on her side by isolating her from France and England. Spain and Belgium and, to a degree, Greece offered chances of alienating France and England.

The aim of France and England during this period was to annihilate the effects of the treaty of Unkiar Iskelessi. At first they threatened to do so by violence. Then they settled down to a long period of observation of the Dardanelles. The manœuvres of their fleets, with Smyrna and the Troad as their bases, became an annual phenomenon. At the same time every effort was made to win the Turks away from their exclusive alliance with Russia. The Porte, while avoiding every outward sign of a break with her powerful neighbor, was not loath to make *sub rosa* advances to encourage the rivalry of the two Western Powers.

Russia had proclaimed her right of exclusive intervention in Turkey. This right was at once denied by France and England, and Russia herself limited this right by voluntary agreement with the essential ally, Austria. It became the diplomatic aim of the London and Paris cabinets to bring the Eastern Question into the concert of Europe, in a word, to require Russia to submit her claims on Constantinople to a conference or entente of the Powers. This Russia refused to do. She stubbornly refused to communicate to France and England the Münchengrätz agreement. That would have allowed the latter to comment on it, to enter into diplomatic communications binding the freedom of Russia's future action, or even to adhere to it, thus making the Münchengrätz agreement a

European obligation. But the idea of a conference held on stubbornly in men's minds in London, Paris and even Vienna. At every moment of stress an effort was likely to be made to subject the "European side" of the Eastern Question to a conference of the Powers.

If Russia refused to be a party to a conference of the Powers on the Eastern Question, she had to be ready to solve that question to her own advantage and by her own forces. In 1829 the solution of the Straits problem in Russia's favor had to be postponed. In 1833 the dimly sketched plan for seizing the Bosphorus gave way to the self-contradictory and, at bottom, useless treaty of Unkiar Iskelessi. In 1838 Russia was ready to repeat the exploit of 1833. Her forces were marshalled on the northern shore of the Black Sea; her fleet was ready to make the dash from Sevastopol.

III

Russian Military Plans in 1838

Up to the beginning of July, 1838, there was nothing in Palmerston's conduct to suggest that he would not welcome the decisive struggle between Russia and England over the Straits. He had refrained from discussing possible contingencies with the Russian ambassador, Count Pozzo di Borgo. He had not invited Russia to join the centre of entente which had been under discussion for the past month between London, Paris, and Vienna. Did Palmerston hope that Metternich could be persuaded to exclude Russia from the discussions of the Eastern Question, thus drawing Austria into an anti-Russian coalition? Or was the English foreign secretary waiting to see if Metternich, in the conferences to be held at Toeplitz, might not bring Russia to sacrifice her jealously safeguarded right of separate intervention in Turkey?

In any case, Pozzo di Borgo, moulded by the heroic spirit of the Napoleonic wars, and convinced of Palmerston's unalterable hostility to Russia in every sphere of the political struggle, was hoping for a different outcome of the conferences which were to be opened in the Bohemian watering-place.[1] Europe was about to be thrown into turmoil by Mohamed Ali's declaration of independence. Russia would then promptly seize the Straits with sufficient force to hold the Sultan to

[1] See Appendix B.

the alliance with Russia and to prevent a surprise attack by England and France against the Russian fortified position there. England and France, realizing their inability to reopen the European side of the Eastern Question—the Straits—would turn to quarrelling with each other for the friendship and favor of the new sovereign of Egypt and Syria. Austria would surely not commit the fatal mistake of opposing Russia's policy. "Since the Turkish Empire is bound to be dissolved, her [Austria's] policy ought to lead her to arrange for herself the occasion of making some useful acquisitions and to maintain her alliance with Russia. The Emperor's wisdom will bring about that understanding today, when the Sovereigns and Cabinets are assembled."

For Pozzo di Borgo, then, the Toeplitz meeting was to prepare the way for an active policy of Austro-Russian cooperation in the Eastern Question. These two Powers were not to an equal degree able to exercise influence over European Turkey nor equally eager to make "useful acquisitions." With all her active forces concentrated on the surveillance of her Italian possessions, of the insidious activities of the German liberal movement, and of the increasingly turbulent manifestations of Hungarian national demands, Austria, weakened by her overload of debt, and divided in council between Kolowrat and Metternich, was not ready for an active policy in the Balkans. Her attitude of passive resistance to change made Austria rather an ally of the Powers which feared and resisted Russian advance to the Straits. But in restraining Russian zeal to be first at the death-bed of the "sick man," Metternich could not show his hand.   He could not uncover the threat of a European conference, which would turn against Russia if Nicolas should prove unwilling to sacrifice his special rights regarding Turkey and to subordinate his actions to those of the concert of Europe.   It may be inferred that Metternich did not press his proposal to invite to Toeplitz the English ambassador at Vienna.   That would have shocked the feelings of the Emperor Nicolas, accustomed as he was to regard these family gatherings of the three absolute monarchs of Europe as political manifestations against the free-thinking West.   Even without the presence of an English ambassador at Toeplitz, it was assumed that all its actions and discussions would shortly become known at London and Paris.[2]

The diplomatic tension was intensified by a resurgence of the Polish revolutionary activity both within the Polish provinces and among the emigration.   On leaving St. Petersburg for Germany, Nicolas had been obliged to change his route because of the discovery of a new Polish plot in Vilna.   At Warsaw he had abandoned the plan, urged by the Viceroy, Paskievich, of making a speech to that city's inhabitants.   His visit was confined to the citadel, with its guns trained ominously on Warsaw itself.[3]   The Emperor's lightning-like trips about the city were guarded by long lines of soldiery.   The manœuvres held near Warsaw were regarded by the rest of Europe as a pretext for

[2] P. G. Divov, "Dnevnik," *Russk. Star.*, 1902, CX, 640.

[3] Paul Lacroix, *Histoire de la vie et du règne de Nicolas I,* 8 vols., Paris, 1864-73, VII, 43-45.

concentrating large masses of troops where they would
serve as a warning to Europe, in case of opposition to
Russian policy. "Only fear, in my opinion, acts on
the Poles," thus Nicolas summed up his inspection of
Poland.[4] Under the impression of these revolutionary
dangers at home, Nicolas probably was satisfied with
inspiring Europe with the spectacle of the intimacy
and union of the three conservative sovereigns, in
Toeplitz. Even in that watering-place, with its holi-
day crowd and idyllic atmosphere, the public was un-
pleasantly impressed by the elaborate precautions
taken to ensure the safety of the Russian Emperor.[5]
Conversations among the rulers and their ministers
were concerned with the progress of the Belgian question towards a settlement, with the determination of
the attitude of the three Eastern Powers towards the
cause of Don Carlos in Spain, with the repression of
the Polish revolutionary movement in their respective
provinces and in the Free City of Cracow. In addition to these weighty continental problems, a place had
to be made for the Egyptian question. Metternich and
Nicolas came to a complete agreement. The versatile
Austrian chancellor had so far turned his back on his
close friends of the month before that he called Palmerston's plan for sending Austrian troops to Asia
Minor "a monstrous idea," and laughed at the English
minister's ignorance of geography.[6] Martens, somewhat gratuitously, concludes: "The Cabinet of Vienna

[4] Kn. Shcherbatov, *General fel'dmarshal knyaz' Paskievich, ego
zhizn' i deyatel'nost'*, 6 vols., St. Petersburg, 1888-1904, V, 365.

[5] Baronne du Montet, *Souvenirs 1785-1866*, Paris, 1904, p. 335.

[6] Metternich to Nesselrode, private, August 2, 1838, F. F. Martens, *Recueil, etc.*, IV, pt. 1, 478-479.

appeared openly hostile to the English government and seemed determined to follow Russia's policy step by step." [7]   In any case, Metternich had lost his fear of an aggressive Russian action for this year at least. Touched by the invocation of the Münchengrätz agreement of 1833, he sent a despatch to his consul-general in Alexandria, almost identical in terms with that despatched by Nesselrode from Toeplitz.[8]   As a result of the Toeplitz meetings, the Russian Vice-Chancellor could now draw up his reply to Mohamed Ali's declaration of May 25.   It was in the main a reiteration of the Russian advice and menaces of the preceding March.   It welcomed any measures taken by France and England against the Pasha of Egypt, and invited the other Powers to deliver simultaneous and identical declarations to the Pasha of Egypt.   By implication it rejected all collective decisions or steps which might rob Russia of her freedom of action in the Straits.   It reaffirmed Russia's determination, in case of unjust aggression by the Pasha, to render any assistance demanded by the Sultan, her ally.   This was a notice to the Pasha of Egypt and to the Powers of Europe that Russia would insist on the execution of the treaty of Unkiar Iskelessi.   In other words, if a situation like that of 1833 again arose, Russia would once more occupy the Straits.

The news received at Toeplitz was not encouraging. Mohamed Ali had declared to the Russian consul-general that he was determined to proclaim his inde-

---

[7] *Ibid.*, p. 478.

[8] R. A., Struve to Nesselrode, 26 July/2 August [*sic*], 1838, Vienna, folio 217, No. 47.

pendence in any case; if the Powers supported his plea
to the Sultan, he would make pecuniary sacrifices to
satisfy his sovereign; if the Powers refused to aid
him, he would attain the same goal by renouncing his
position as vassal and adopting an attitude of defense.
The Russian agent, Medem, was convinced that the
Pasha's determination was set, and that there was little
hope for peace.[9]   This threatening news could not
have relieved Nicolas's premonition of early and probably decisive action in Turkey.   He wrote on this
despatch: "It is very unpromising, and the future
seems to me very uncertain; but we are ready." [10]

The Emperor Nicolas at all times had an expeditionary force at Sevastopol, ready to be ferried across
to the Bosphorus.   In the meantime, these troops were
used for completing the fortifications of Russia's great
naval base in the Crimea.   Since 1830 those works had
progressed rapidly.   The absence of free labor and
the scarcity of money in the treasury made it urgent
for the government to use its conscript troops for the
work of fortifying and building.   But such occupa-
tions were never allowed to interfere with keeping the
military training of the men at top-notch.   In 1837
General Muraviev had been very harshly removed
from the command of the expeditionary troops because they did not come up to the very severe standard
set by the "Tsar-parade-master."

The Black Sea fleet was likewise kept up to its full

[9] R. A., A. Medem to Nesselrode, Alexandria, 16/28 June 1838,
folio 1, No. 8, received at Toeplitz.

[10] "C'est bien louche, et l'avenir me paraît bien incertain; mais
nous sommes prêts."

fighting power. It had two tasks to fulfill. It had to keep up communications along the eastern shore of the Black Sea, among the Russian forts on the Abkhasian coast. These forts were isolated from one another by land. It also had to keep the mountaineers from receiving arms and munitions from the English smugglers. The latter made their centre at Trebizond and ignored the Russian prohibition of trade with the ports of the eastern end of the Black Sea, except Redout-Kalé. It was only in 1837 that the house of Messrs. Bell and Company had protested against the Russian blockade of the Caucasian coast. In the seizure of the "Vixen" by the Russian navy, the English government seemed for a time to see a convenient diplomatic excuse to deny the effectiveness of the Russian cordon around the Caucasus. Eventually, willingness on both sides to avoid a collision led to a compromise settlement, which decided nothing.

The other task of the Black Sea fleet was to have its squadrons ready to leave at any time for the Bosphorus. Any delay in the execution of such sailing orders might nullify the geographical advantage which Russia possessed over the French and British fleets. At the same time the Emperor followed with the greatest attention the improvements made in steam navigation. The rough winds of the Euxine, famous since the days of the Golden Fleece, might destroy Russia's advantage of geographical proximity to the Straits. Really adequate steam navigation on the other hand would remove that danger. Five days before his arrival at Toeplitz, Nicolas wrote to Prince Menshikov, his minister of marine, that an agent had returned from America with important news about steam navigation. At Toeplitz he would decide whether it would not be well to despatch him directly to America, to purchase and bring back one of the perfected steamboats.[11]

One of the greatest impediments to the development of the Russian military marine was the unwillingness of the Russian peasants to follow the sea. In order to force the training of Russian subjects in navigation, it was required that all Russian ships engaged in foreign trade must have crews at least 50 percent Russian in citizenship.[12] But this law could not be applied without having an effect the opposite of that intended. It merely served to discourage navigation under the Russian flag. At the beginning of 1839 the Imperial Government was obliged to exempt from this general rule for another seven years all Russian ships departing from the Baltic ports.[13] Along the Black Sea coast even more energetic measures had to be taken, to provide a minimum number of sea-faring men. In 1834 self-governing and free societies of sailors were permitted in Nikopol and Aleshki.[14] In 1839 this measure was extended to all towns and trading hamlets along the coasts of the Black and Azov Seas and up the banks of the Dnieper River. A second part of the same decree reads: "In order to increase the number of experienced Russian sea-farers and to

[11] Nicolas to Prince A. S. Menshikov, 2/14 July 1838, Fischbach, *Russk. Star.*, XC, 232.

[12] *Collection of Laws*, Art. 589.

[13] *Zhurn. Manufaktur i Torgovli*, 1839, II, 190-191, decree No. 28.

[14] *Collection of Laws*, Appendix, XI, 595.

form a class, hitherto unknown in Russia, of sailors, it is permitted to establish free sailor societies in the villages belonging to the state in that district, freeing them from all servile and peasant dues and allowing them to elect their own elders." [15]   Even this, in appearance, advantageous opening for advancement and emancipation was regarded by the state peasants with great suspicion.   The rumor was started that the peasants were bound to serve on shipboard for life; that their privileges were only illusory; that their families would be exiled from the villages where they had so far lived.   It was only the personal persuasion of Count Vorontsov, governor of Novorossia, and the paternal solicitude of Vice-Admiral Lazarev which led to the creation of thirty-five of these sailor societies. And even by the beginning of 1841 only 252 men were supplied from them for the fleet.   But the author of the article in the official journal was enthusiastic about the new institution.   "Everywhere commercial navigation is inseparable from military, . . . everywhere they live as with one life.   In a word, the establishment of a class of sailors is the foundation of our future mastery of the seas." [16]   As so often in Russian history the understanding of an innovation outran the capacity to make it of practical significance.

These measures could be only of long-term effect. Yet they showed what efforts the Russian government had to make in order to ensure an adequate development of mercantile and naval power on the Black Sea. In 1838, however, immediate steps had to be taken to

[15] *Zhurn. Manufak. i Torgovli,* 1839, IV, 345-351.
[16] *Zhurn. Manufak. i Torgovli,* 1841, II, 438-453.

make sure that Russia would not be left unprepared by any unexpected events in Turkey. The news of the Pasha's threat to declare his independence reached Nicolas in Silesia, shortly after the manœuvres near Warsaw and a week before the opening of the conferences in Toeplitz. His first thought was for the condition of the future "army in Turkey." Paskievich, the viceroy of Poland and the Emperor's "father commander," as he called him with almost filial affection, drew up a memorandum of what was required for the expedition. Nicolas wrote to Paskievich on July 15 that he had already given instructions to the Minister of War, Count Chernyshev, to have the 5th Infantry Corps, at Sevastopol, ready to move at the first command. The projected union of the French and English fleets made him suspect an attempt to force the Dardanelles and surprise Constantinople before the Russian forces and fleet could reach there. The 2nd Corps was also to be ready to go by sea, to reinforce the 5th Corps, and the 3rd was to be ready to occupy Moldavia and Wallachia, with the cavalry, to ensure communication by land with the expeditionary force in Constantinople and to be available as a reserve. Nicolas gloated at the thought of his power. "Then let England and France stew, we are ready." Russia's real security lay in the unpreparedness of England and France. England had only 40,000 troops available, for most of her land forces were massed in Canada, to keep down the rebellion and to ward off a possible attack by the United States.[17]

[17] Shcherbatov, *op. cit.*, V, 365-366; and Nicolas to Menshikov, 2/14 July 1838, Fischbach, *Russk. Star.*, XC, 232.

From St. Petersburg the necessary steps were already being taken. A mobile commissary column was being organized at Kherson, to follow the 5th Corps from Sevastopol across the Black Sea. Its men and artillery were being brought to full completeness. Defective weapons were to be exchanged. Its commander, General Lieders, had been informed by a confidential, oral communication, of what lay ahead. Chernyshev agreed with Paskievich that it would be inadvisable to occupy the Danubian Principalities. That would arouse the suspicion of Austria and of the Sultan himself; at the same time that region would not be suitable for filling out the army's stores.[18] "The occupation of the fortified points at the mouth of the Bosphorus, on both its shores, must constitute, in my opinion, the absolute and chief condition of any assistance on our part, and if the Porte rejected it, being menaced by the united fleets of France and England, then nothing would be left for us to do except to seize the Bosphorus by force of arms in order to guarantee our navigation of the Black Sea and the security of our own shores."[19]

There was no doubt then in the mind of the Emperor or of his military advisors but that the Russian fleet and landing-force could seize the Bosphorus either with or without the consent of the Turks. Barante,

---

[18] The Danubian Principalities were under close surveillance. As early as July 5 the English chargé d'affaires at St. Petersburg asked Nesselrode's substitute, Divov, about the significance of the assembling of large stores of supplies in Moldavia (Divov, "Dnevnik," *Russk. Star.,* 1902, CX, 641).

[19] *Sbornik Imp. Ross. Ist. Obshchestva,* St. Petersburg, 1905, CXXII, 383-385.

French ambassador to Russia, was also convinced of this, as well as Marshal Marmont, Duke of Ragusa, who had recently made careful studies both of southern Russia and of Turkey. He felt that Russia could take Constantinople and even the Dardanelles "the minute the Ottoman Empire fell." [20]   Marmont also pointed out that Russia could not hold the Straits unless she also possessed the three provinces of Moldavia, Wallachia, and Bulgaria. The interruption of Russia's line of land communications would force her to evacuate Constantinople. Paskievich also clearly visualized the eventual danger from Austria. Russia's program should be to occupy an impregnable position on the shores of the Bosphorus, and then to stand on the defensive.

Russia was able at that time to send the 5th and 3rd infantry corps into Turkey. That meant 80,000 men under arms. After spying out the ground in September, 1838, the French Ambassador reported that Russia could send 20,000 men in summer and 10,000 in winter to seize Constantinople.[21] This discrepancy between the Russian and French figures is explained by Barante's failure to include Kherson, with its important military settlements. He saw only Sevastopol, where the 5th corps was working to complete the new fortifications, while waiting for the campaign to open. But even 10,000 men, Barante felt, would be a force ample for seizing Constantinople, especially since that

[20] Maréchal de Marmont, *Mémoires,* 9 vols., Paris, 1857, IX, 139-156.

[21] Baron A. G. P. B. Barante, *Souvenirs,* 8 vols., Paris, 1890-91, VI, 122-141; Barante to Molé, October 19, 1838.

capital was quite unfortified from the side of the Black
Sea. The remedy which he proposed for this dangerous situation was to establish an encampment of British
and French troops within striking distance of the
Dardanelles, in perpetual readiness to act against
Russia. The mere hint of such a plan would probably
have brought the Russians to the Bosphorus.

But Russia was not concerned solely with the possibility of military action in the Straits. "The hostile
disposition of the French and English cabinets" towards Russia and "the general state of Europe" convinced Chernyshev that Russia could not spare more
than 80,000 men for the Straits. Any further increases
in the expeditionary force would weaken the armies
which Russia must always have available on her western frontier. That meant that Russia was bound to
be particularly interested at this time in the military
power of her two allies, Prussia and Austria, and of
the German Confederation. Once Russia held the
Straits, France would have to cross Germany to attack
her, and while the numerical and military preponderance
of France over Germany had been weakened since
Napoleonic times, it was still great enough for Europe
to look with anxiety on the efforts of the France of
the July Monarchy to reach the Rhine. The renewal
of interest in the Belgian question, since March 1838,
when the King of Holland had offered to accept the
24 articles, reminded Europe of French patronage of
Belgium and of France's own desire, admitted by
Perier and Talleyrand, of incorporating those provinces with France. It was not impossible, therefore,
that the Eastern Question might take acute form at

just this time and be turned into a continental war in which France would aim to reach the Rhine frontier.

Under these conditions the Emperor Nicolas took a special interest in strengthening Germany's defenses against France. His cure in the Bohemian resort was punctuated by reviews of Austrian troops. In Bavaria he inspected the garrisons of Munich and Augsburg. He waxed enthusiastic over the new artillery of the Zoller system. He was indignant at the indifference of the art-loving Bavarian king for the appearance and training of his army.[22] Nicolas's attitude towards the German rulers, allied to him by family ties and by a reluctantly admitted community of political principles, was greatly resented by them. After the Kalisch manœuvres of 1835 he had strongly urged the King of Bavaria to improve the cadres of his army. In case of war it would be a part of the vanguard of the great force, in which the Russian army would be the reserve. The rulers of Germany, far from being flattered at the prospect of being sacrificed as the vanguard of the Russian army, resented the assumption that their political choice had been made and consecrated once and for all. Even the aged and venerated King of Prussia was more than a little ruffled at the assumption, made by his Russian son-in-law, that the Prussian army, although considerably inferior to the Russian in external discipline, was still good enough to take the first line of defense against France.[23]

[22] Nicolas to Paskievich, Kreuth, 10/22 August 1838, Shcherbatov, *op. cit.*, V, 368-369.

[23] "Rossia i Germania v XIX veke," *Russk. Star.*, 1898, VC, 7.

The able soldier king of Würtemberg was much more to Nicolas's liking. The Emperor visited him at his summer estate at Friedrichshafen. "The King depicted to the Emperor his present position in Germany and the rôle which he would take in case of a French invasion. . . . That is one good result achieved then. Later, the Emperor handed him Prince Metternich's memorandum on the four federal fortresses. . . . The Emperor takes a great interest in the construction of a federal fortress without as yet having, so it seemed to me, a definite idea as to the most suitable point." [24]   Here is a picture of the Russian Emperor using his family influence among the smaller states of the German Confederation to put through the plan for federal fortifications which had been promised after the Congress of Vienna, but which was still unexecuted in 1838. It was not carried out until the war scare of 1840. Even Sweden, insignificant as it seemed in a military sense, was not left out of Nicolas's sphere of action. A surprise visit to the aged king, in June, 1838, although it led to a demonstration against Russia in the streets of Stockholm, was alleged to have revived the old bonds of friendship between the two governments. It was intended to give Palmerston cause for thought.

The alarm caused in European cabinets by Mohamed Ali's threats led, therefore, to an examination and mustering of the forces available. Russia was prepared "to the last cartridge" to act against Constantinople, either at the request of the Sultan, or despite

[24] Peter von Meiendorff, *Politischer und privater briefwechsel,* 1826-1863, 3 vols., Berlin, 1923, I, 66-68.

him, if France and England turned their fleets towards the Dardanelles. At the same time Russia was anxious not to offend Austria, and wanted to have the German Confederation ready to receive the first shock of the attack, if France and England, baffled at the Straits, should start a continental war against the empire of Nicolas I.

Meanwhile, the immediate danger of war in the East had been allayed. That war of Russia against France and England seemed to the cautious Nesselrode "the most unfavorable of all wars"; even the militant Pozzo di Borgo, with his fiery Corsican imagination, felt that the crisis which would follow the dissolution of the Ottoman Empire would be "a fearful trial." That test of strength was averted for the time being. The Pasha of Egypt, impressed by the unanimous threats uttered by the Powers against his bold claims, decided to postpone his declaration of independence till less stormy times.

IV

Franco-Russian Relations and the Eastern Question

In 1838 Nicolas I believed that his forces were fully prepared to carry through a decisive military action in Turkey. But the occupation of the Bosphorus, whether with or without the consent of the Sultan, would certainly provoke a counter-offensive, both diplomatic and military, on the part of France and England. Was it not possible, however, to diminish the danger of concerted action by the two Western Powers through skillful playing upon the many sources of disagreement between Paris and London?

The "entente cordiale" had been formed shortly after the revolutionary events of 1830 had upset the European scheme of things, so laboriously put together in 1815. It had been strengthened by French fear of the three conservative Powers of Eastern Europe. By 1835, however, the division of Europe into two camps had resulted in a dead-lock. This encouraged each Power to look once more to its material interests, once it was clearly grasped that Louis Philippe's opportunist policy furnished the best bulwark against the dangers of French revolutionary policy in Europe. The king of Prussia risked the indignation of Nicolas I in order to aid Louis Philippe in breaking down the marriage boycott against the Orléans family. Metternich after 1835 carried on a secret correspondence with Louis Philippe and affected great respect for his sagacity. While French relations with the two German Powers were improving, relations with England were growing worse. In Spain French diplomacy was backing the Moderados, while England favored the Progressistas, the more radical party of the urban bourgeoisie. In Greece Palmerston was pressing a constitution upon King Otto, while France was willing to continue financial assistance to the new government without requiring any radical changes. In the Belgian question, England had swung as early as May, 1838, into a position unfavorable to extreme Belgian claims. Louis Philippe, while urging moderation in Brussels, was unwilling to leave Leopold in the lurch. During the summer of 1838 the representatives of the four Powers in the London conference, turning a cold shoulder to French representations, drew up the terms of the final settlement between Holland and Belgium. When the treaties were at last signed in April, 1839, Anglo-French cordiality had been severely strained. Palmerston had accustomed both Austria and Russia to cooperate with England over a period of nearly a year. A major issue had been settled in a way damaging to French prestige. The strained relations between Paris and London affected Russia's position in the Eastern Question in two diverse ways. During 1838 they created in the French government an unreciprocated inclination to go in step with Russia in the Turko-Egyptian question, in order to offset its practical isolation in the Belgian conference. In 1839, on the other hand, the English ministry welcomed Russian cooperation in the settlement of the Eastern

Question, because the Belgian struggle had shown that where Russian and English interests coincided, supposed questions of principle could very quickly be thrust aside.

During the summer of 1838 a vague scheme of Franco-Russian cooperation in the Egyptian question was felt in the air. That cooperation had a certain natural basis in the position of the two Powers. Fundamentally, Russia had no objection to the independence of the Pasha of Egypt. It might even be advantageous for her, since the more the Porte had to fear its neighbor to the south, the more eagerly it would cling to its dangerous friend on the north. France felt certain objections to Russia's possessing the Straits, but she was attracted by one prospective advantage. There would then be three Powers in the Mediterranean. France would not have to face British sea-power alone there; at times there could be an advantageous combination of two against one. And if Russia's possession of the Straits brought with it the strengthening of the Pasha of Egypt, France could have no complaint. No French communications with the east were jeopardized by the growing power of the Viceroy. Moreover, France and Egypt were in a similar juridical position with regard to the Porte. To all effects, Algeria, a dependency of the Ottoman Empire, was becoming a French colony as fast as it was being conquered. The Pasha of Egypt also held lands which for many decades had been independent of the actual control of the Porte; at the same time he was bound to the Sultan in terms of suzerainty. Both France and Egypt suffered from this anomalous position, Egypt more than France, of course. The protest of the French ambassador, in June, 1838, against the departure of the Turkish fleet for its annual cruise illustrated this community of interest. Admiral Roussin objected to the fleet's taking the direction either of Tunis or of Egypt.[1]

This vague community of interest between Russia, France and Egypt was clearly sensed by Palmerston in 1838. Upon the first reception of the news of Mohamed Ali's intention to proclaim his independence, as relayed from Paris in the first week of June, Palmerston at once hit upon a plan for restraining the Pasha from this step, so fraught with danger for the peace of Europe. A collective step by the Powers would have the double advantage of imposing obedience on the Pasha and of binding the action of each Power. Russia would then no longer be free to act for her own purposes in Turkey. A second possibility was that England and France could make a convention to support Turkey against Egypt. But he had doubts as to what France really wanted to do. Palmerston added, in his letter to Granville of June 8, 1838: "It must not be forgotten that one great danger to Europe is the possibility of a combination between France and Russia, which, although prevented at present by the personal feelings of the Emperor, may not always be as impossible as it is now; and it would be well to fix the policy of France in the right

[1] R. A., Rückmann to Nesselrode, Constantinople, 4/16 June, 1838, folio 48, No. 92.

track with respect to affairs of the Levant while we have the power to do so." [2]

This danger to English interests from Franco-Russian cooperation in the eastern Mediterranean was greater at this time than before or later under Louis Philippe. The Emperor Nicolas and Nesselrode highly approved of the conservative policy of Count Molé. They signified in a number of despatches their sympathy for his attempts to enlarge the royal prerogative in France and to reduce the power of the Chambers. They appreciated his unwillingness to see Palmerston force a constitution on Greece, even though they condemned as small-hearted his refusal to take a stand four-square on the conservative platform. Nicolas's expressions about Louis Philippe were much more favorable at this time than before or after. In October 1837 the French ambassador in Petersburg, Barante, wrote to his colleague in Berlin: "Abroad, at least where I am, the reputation of the King for wisdom and firmness is progressing every day. . . . There is satisfaction in representing France." [3] Even in London it was suspected that Nicolas was inclined to court Louis Philippe. Raikes wrote in his journal, on July 13, 1838, that the Emperor "met Horace Vernet at Berlin, and launched out into such praise of the King's conduct that Vernet asked if he might repeat them to his sovereign, which the other readily

2 Baron Henry Lytton Bulwer, *Life of Henry John Temple, Viscount Palmerston,* 3 vols., London, 1871-74, II, 269.

3 Paul Thureau-Dangin, *Histoire de la Monarchie de Juillet,* 7 vols., Paris, 1888-92, III, 274.

assented to." [4]   On June 14, 1838, Vernet had an
audience of Louis Philippe, directly after his return
from Berlin.[5]

The first conversations on the Eastern Question in
June, 1838, gave indications that Russia and France
could cooperate in its solution.   Louis Philippe promised to use his influence to restrain the Pasha of Egypt.
He hoped that Russia would use its influence over the
Porte, in case the Pasha did proclaim his independence, to persuade it to refrain from beginning hostilities, and to leave it to the four Powers to arrange
a settlement of the dispute.[6]   This seemingly innocuous suggestion deserves to be examined, for in it
lies the germ of French policy during the next three
years of the Eastern Question.   If the declaration of
independence did come, then the Powers were not to
attack the Pasha of Egypt and force him to come
to terms favorable for the Porte.   On the contrary,
the Porte was to be restrained from using force against
its vassal.   In other words, time would be allowed to
lapse; the Porte would despair of ever reducing its
vassal to submission and eventually would agree to
allow Mohamed Ali to keep all the territories which he
possessed at present.   And in suggesting that Russia
should urge this passive course on the Sultan, Louis
Philippe was acting craftily.   If Nesselrode had been
naïve enough to propose this attitude to the Sultan's

    [4] Thomas Raikes, *A portion of the journal kept from 1831 to 1847*,
4 vols., London, 1861, III, 278.

    [5] J. Taschereau, ed., *Revue rétrospective; ou, archives secrets du
dernier gouvernement* . . ., Paris, 1848, p. 98.

    [6] R. A., Medem to Nesselrode, Paris, 25 May/6 June, 1838, folio
169, No. 45.

government, the Russo-Turkish alliance would have ceased to exist from that very moment. On the other hand, if the Pasha of Egypt knew, and he was sure to know, that at least two Powers—France and Russia —were urging the Porte not to take up arms in case he declared his independence, he would not have hesitated another day in declaring it.

This apparent inclination to court Russia's support in the Egyptian question was partly due to French suspicion of the activity of English agents like Waghorn and Bowring in Egypt. Molé was much relieved when Granville was able to assure him positively that the British government by no means shared the opinions expressed by those agents.[7]

The instructions sent by Molé to Roussin at Constantinople on June 11 expressed this French desire to prepare the way for the reception of the Egyptian declaration of independence with the least commotion possible. Roussin was instructed to urge the Porte not to make the declaration of independence a motive of rupture, but to allow the Powers to settle his dispute with the disobedient vassal. In other words, France hoped that if the Pasha did declare his independence, the Sultan would remain quiescent, for if he resorted, and unsuccessfully, to violence, the Powers might be forced to intervene to protect the Porte.[8]

A few days later the French conception had taken more definite form. Molé agreed with the English

[7] R. A., Medem to Nesselrode, Paris, 8/20 June, 1838, folio 169, No. 52.

[8] R. A., Medem to Nesselrode, Paris, 1/13 June, 1838, folio 169, No. 49.

cabinet that it was desirable to send English and French squadrons to restrain the Pasha. At the same time he observed that it would be advantageous to prepare the Sultan to make a concession which would satisfy Mohamed Ali's pretensions. "It meant assuring to Ibrahim Pasha the succession in the government of the provinces possessed at present by his father. In communicating this idea, the President of the Council (Molé) said to me that he was not making it the object of a proposal, but of a mere confidence as to the most certain way of avoiding a rupture which the Pasha will not cease provoking so long as he has not assured to his family the inheritance which he wishes at any price to leave to it." [9]   A few days later Molé was stressing a different side of the problem. The Powers should guarantee the settlement of Kutaya. That was what the Pasha had originally asked for in March. That guarantee would enable both sides to disarm. Molé was influenced in favor of this compromise by Palmerston's preference for maintaining the *status quo* of Kutaya.[10]

The difference between the French and English attitudes was aptly seized by the Russian ambassador in London, who had had many years of service in both capitals. "King Philippe is aiming at what seems impossible of attainment, namely: the condescension and the submission of the Sultan to the sudden steps

[9] R. A., Medem to Nesselrode, Paris, 4/16 June, 1838, folio 169, No. 51.

[10] R. A., Medem to Nesselrode, Paris, 8/20 June, 1838, folio 169, No. 52; Pozzo di Borgo to Nesselrode, London, 21 June/3 July, 1838, folio 129, No. 53.

and ambition of Mohamed Ali. The instructions which you inform me have been given on this subject to Admiral Roussin at Constantinople are in my opinion neither prudent nor opportune. Lord Palmerston has held to me the same language which he has repeated in writing to Lord Granville, according to the information which you have been so kind as to give me, M. le Comte. I hope that he will persist in it. Nothing would be more false than the position of France and England in case the Sultan should declare war against the rebel Pasha, violator of the treaty and violator of the most solemn engagements made under the mediation of these same Powers, and in case they should wish to oppose the defense of the rightful sovereign and the assistance which others might perhaps grant him. That prospect is evident, but, on the other hand, Louis Philippe wants peace, even at everyone's expense, and if the Pasha becomes a sovereign without political commotion, he will not fail to say that he owes that great success to him. These truths ought to be foreseen and felt by the English ministry. Unfortunately, it is not certain that it will grasp them by itself . . ." [11]

It was clear, therefore, that Louis Philippe, in pursuance of his "peace at any price" policy, was anxious to prepare the way for a settlement between the Sultan and his vassal, at the expense of the former. In June, 1838, it seemed to the Russian ambassador that England was in danger of being drawn into this policy.

[11] R. A., Pozzo di Borgo to Medem, particulière, London, 5/17 June, 1838, folio 129, ad. No. 54.

He feared that, if a crisis arose, England and France would turn their forces against Russia in the Straits, rather than come to the aid of the Sultan in maintaining the arrangement of Kutaya, negotiated under their mediation in 1833. Such a prospect, though perhaps inconsistent with the respect professed by England and France for the maintenance of the Ottoman Empire, was to an even greater degree dangerous for Russia's freedom of action in the Straits. Meanwhile, France and England were waiting for Russia's declaration of policy in this crisis.

Her policy was formulated at Toeplitz in July, 1838, after Nicolas's conferences with Metternich. It took the form of a declaration to be made to England and France. It was to be made first in London; then, after Pozzo di Borgo had studied its effect there, it was to be forwarded to Paris, which Nicolas affected to put in second place. Its contents were: "1) the simultaneous and identical declarations which our Cabinet proposes to the four other Great Powers to address to the Viceroy of Egypt; 2) the assurance, given by the Emperor, that His Imperial Majesty will view without the slightest suspicion the adoption of any measure, the avowed purpose of which would be to maintain Mohamed Ali in his present relations of vassalage to the Sultan; 3) the announcement of the regrettable, but imperious, necessity, under which Our August Master would be, of intervening Himself in the affairs of Egypt and of granting the aid and assistance which the Sultan could demand of Him if the Pasha of Egypt embarked on an unjust aggression." [12] The purpose of this high-sounding declaration was to spur on England and France to bring to a peaceful solution the quarrel between the Sultan and the Pasha. It reasserted the validity for Russia and Turkey of the treaty of 1833, which England and France had ostentatiously declared could not be regarded as part of European public law. The statement that Russia would interfere in the affairs of Egypt was susceptible of at least two interpretations. It might mean that Russia would again interfere, as in 1833, to save the Sultan's capital from attack. But it might be taken to mean that Russia would interfere actively in Syria to defend the interests of her ally. Whether this ambiguous interpretation was intentional, it is hard to say. On Palmerston it acted as a deliberate challenge. He jumped to the conclusion that Russia was preparing to invade Syria. He tried to open a conference on the Eastern Question by means of a strategem scarcely worthy of his reputation as a statesman. Palmerston's purpose was to present Russia with an unpleasant alternative. Either she would have to subordinate her actions in the Straits to the decisions of a European conference,—a thing which Russia had skillfully avoided so far,—or else Russia would be faced with a united front of France and England and perhaps Austria.

The same declaration of Toeplitz, although communicated with offensive delay to the Paris cabinet, produced a quite different impression there. One rea-

[12] R. A., Medem to Nesselrode, Paris, réservée, 10/22 August, 1838, folio 170, No. 70.

son for that was that French and Russian policies had of late been in much closer accord. Count Molé, hard pressed in maintaining his position against the intrigues of Palmerston and Sébastiani in London, was not sorry to show to Louis Philippe that he understood much better than they how to deal with the eastern problem. In a note to Louis Philippe, dated July 15, 1838, Molé proved that he had foreseen the needs and possibilities of the situation better than had Palmerston. The latter had proposed a collective and common step to be made to the Pasha by the Powers, except Prussia. Molé had rejected that proposal, giving preference to the separate, but similar notes, now proposed by Palmerston in his turn. Molé had foreseen since the first week in June that collective action would never be accepted by Russia. Since the Toeplitz conference was about to open, Molé was equally sure that Metternich could not be drawn now into such a combination, hostile to Russian principles. Even the step proposed by Palmerston, inviting Russia to join her fleet to the French and English squadrons in the Mediterranean and thus to give up her own freedom of action, Molé rejected as unnecessary. Thus, in June and July, 1838, the president of the French council was much closer to the Russian point of view than to Palmerston's. He was anxious, for the sake of the Pasha, to avoid collective steps, which might bind the Powers of Europe in the future arrangement between the Pasha and Sultan. He preferred, like Russia, separate and similar threats. They would intimidate the Pasha of Egypt for that year, but would not make the Porte over-bold or pre-suming.[13]

It was not surprising, therefore, that Count Molé turned a sympathetic ear to the Russian declaration of Toeplitz. To emphasize his own freedom from Palmerston's Russophobia, he read to the Russian chargé d'affaires a report of Sébastiani's, in which the latter entirely agreed with Palmerston's opinion that Russian freedom of action in the Straits must by all means be restricted through the assembling of a conference on the Eastern Question. Molé agreed that the Toeplitz declaration was not provocative, but aimed rather at securing a peaceful solution of the crisis. The Emperor was absolutely justified in announcing that he would not abandon his ally, the Sultan, in case of need. "You have Turkey, as we have Belgium and Spain. They could not be touched without bringing all our interests into play. Instead of thinking merely of prolonging the present state of things, Lord Palmerston is concerned only with the means for diminishing your preponderance in the Orient. The result is that he comes out with the most inconceivable proposals; sometimes it is an Austrian army which he would like to see placed at the disposal of the Porte; again it is a conference through which he wishes to paralyze your action. I predicted to him, just as has happened, that Austria would reject so adventurous a proposal and that Russia would not gratuitously consent to subordinate her action to that of another Power. It is a great mistake in politics to ask of

[13] *Revue rétrospective,* p. 100.

someone else things which you could not grant if you were in that other person's place. Our relations with the English cabinet have enabled me to become convinced how often it sins in this respect, and if, despite the difficulties which arise from that unfortunate tendency, you see us inclined in almost all questions to make common cause with it, that union must be attributed rather to a conformity of institutions and of principles than to a community of interests. Thus, in the affairs of the Orient we cannot attach the same importance as does England to combatting your supremacy; in some cases we would even have many ways of coming to an entente through compensations which you could give us, and, yet, if it became necessary to declare our intentions, I do not hesitate to assert that we should believe ourselves obliged to join a naval demonstration to which England would believe that she had to make up her mind, as against Russia." From this heart-to-heart talk with Molé, the Russian agent drew the following conclusions: ". . . that, if a serious crisis broke out in the Orient and France had to take sides, she would certainly join Great Britain in a demonstration hostile to Russia, but that her action would reflect the lesser importance which she would attach to the result of a struggle in which she would regard her interests as much less engaged than those of her ally, England. If the opinion which I make bold to put forth as to the rôle which France will play in the case in view should seem, Monsieur le Comte, in contradiction with the assurances of a complete neutrality which Louis Philippe has given us on two different occasions, I should beg you to look for the explanation for that in the necessities which will always dominate here the royal will. . . ." The Russian agent felt that the King was sincere in his promises, but that Count Molé was a better judge of what was possible for a French cabinet in its foreign policy.[14]

There is no evidence to explain on what two occasions Louis Philippe had promised the Russian emperor that he would keep France neutral in case of a war between England and Russia. Perhaps one of those times occurred during the "Vixen" crisis of 1837, a time when Nicolas had been particularly well inclined towards Louis Philippe.[15] In any case this conversation between Molé and Medem deserves attention. At this time France was being bitterly attacked by England in her interests in Belgium and Spain. The French cabinet was isolated in the London conference on the Belgian question through Palmerston's ignoring the French ambassador in his negotiations with the three Eastern Powers. Molé's personal position was endangered by the intrigues carried on by Palmerston and Sébastiani. Of all French premiers since 1830 Molé was the one whose principles were most approved by both Austria and Russia. His acknowledgment that Russia and France had a community of interest in the Eastern Question was a direct bid for an entente. If Russia could give France the moral support in European affairs which she had been obliged since 1830 to seek from England, the

---

[14] R. A., Medem to Nesselrode, réservée, Paris, 10/22 August, 1838, folio 170, No. 70.

[15] Thureau-Dangin, *op. cit.*, III, 274.

two cabinets could come to an understanding in the
Eastern Question. Such an understanding could lead
to the satisfaction of both French and Russian ambitions, at the expense of England.

This "feeler" was left without reply from the Russian side. Perhaps the despatch came at an unfortunate
time. Nesselrode and the Emperor Nicolas were travel-
ing in different parts of Germany and did not meet
again until towards the end of September. By then
the Persian difficulties occupied all the attention of
the Russian cabinet. At the same time, Russia was
directly engaged on the English side of the Belgian
question both through her alliance with Austria and
Prussia and through her financial dependence on
England, and she must have felt that the price of a
problematical entente with France on the Eastern Question would be some support of France in the stormy
Belgian conference then going on in London. At the
same time the French premier had confessed that
France would be unable to resist the necessity for
acting in common with England in case of war against
Russia. That might be regarded as a bid for Russia
to remove that one-sided dependence of French foreign
policy which had continued since 1830. But such a
confession might at the same time persuade Russia
that any sacrifices for the sake of French support were
bound to be useless in a crisis. There is one more
possibility. The despatch in question bears none of
the usual signs of having been read by the Emperor.
It is possible that the guiding heads of the Russian
foreign ministry, being resolutely set against France,
did not forward that despatch to the Emperor. It

was well known that the remaining partisans of the traditional Franco-Russian entente, including Pozzo di Borgo, were bitterly fought by the dominant group, made up of Nesselrode, Brunnow, and Polenov. That group believed that Russia must conciliate England and that relying on France to counteract English sea and colonial power would be leaning on a very slender reed. Nicolas himself did not believe in the stability of the French régime. He was convinced of its inability to carry on a strong and independent foreign policy. He did believe in England's strength and therefore in 1839-1840 he sought for an entente in London, not in Paris.

One Russian diplomat of the old school who believed in the advantage of a Russo-French entente was Pozzo di Borgo. From 1815 to 1834 he had been ambassador in France, from which he had driven his bitter enemy, that other and greater Corsican. At the time of his recall from Paris, at the end of 1834, he had been active in working for a Franco-Russian understanding on eastern affairs.[16] Nicolas was unwilling to envisage that possibility and this factor contributed to Pozzo di Borgo's withdrawal from that capital, which he loved with an affection which his exile in London only intensified, and to which he returned to die in 1842. Pozzo di Borgo was much struck by Molé's conversation with the Russian chargé d'affaires regarding the Toeplitz declaration. "By his language the President of the Council [Count Molé] shows that he is far from entering into any collective step or measure;

16 F. F. Martens, *Recueil, etc.,* XV, 158-159.

it is advantageous to maintain him in that determination. . . . Lord Palmerston and General Sébastiani are acting in agreement against us and against Count Molé, whom they have worked so hard to remove from the ministry and from the direction of affairs; there is a constant intrigue between them despite Louis Philippe. As for the eventualities of which the President of the Council has spoken, in case of war, they should not surprise us, but what he says still leaves chances of being able to weaken the cooperation of France with England and even of making her change over, if events allowed that, by using the dexterity which circumstances will demand." [17]

In October, 1838, Pozzo di Borgo returned to his theme with new fire. Palmerston had just delivered to him a long oral manifesto. He complained of the growth of the Russian fleet, he denounced the Russian conquest of the Caucasus, he brought out of the dark closet the skeleton of the Russian threat to India. Pozzo di Borgo had replied with equal firmness and greater calm, and looked forward to the new year with the greatest alarm. In reviewing Russia's diplomatic situation, he felt that Austria was inclining more and more to an understanding with England on eastern affairs, thus renewing her natural policy, which had been broken off by the revolutionary events of 1830. The new treaty of commerce between England and Austria contained a clause which seemed to challenge Russia's control of the mouths of the Danube and therefore had been received with jubilation in London.

[17] R. A., Pozzo di Borgo to Nesselrode, London, 26 August/7 September, 1838, folio 129, No. 83.

At a moment of deep crisis with England and of Austrian hesitation, he felt that Russia needed to examine her relations with France. "As I have already had the occasion, Monsieur le Comte, to observe to the Imperial Cabinet, the English Government cannot avoid the conviction that it is unable to attempt serious attacks and even more unable to accomplish its designs against Russia without France's cooperation. A war which it might undertake in isolation without an evident national motive, would be difficult for it to carry through; a vague jealousy would not suffice for obtaining the sacrifices which it would require. As for France's cooperation, it seems to me impossible to make any anticipations because of the almost complete absence of relations between us and that Power. There is, however, one truth about which it would be dangerous to deceive ourselves, namely: that France against us would put an immense force into the scales. The question, Monsieur le Comte, is very real." [18] This plea, like that of the more youthful and modest Medem in Paris, was left without reply in St. Petersburg.

Russian policy aimed at separating France from England by skillful manœuvering in questions in which those two Powers held contradictory interests. By secret assistance to the reactionary cause in Spain, Russia expected to embitter relations between the two rival Powers backing the Liberal and Progressive causes. By adopting the apparent French willingness to aid Greece without exacting a constitution, Nesselrode

[18] R. A., Pozzo di Borgo to Nesselrode, London, 11/23 October, 1838, folio 130, No. 93.

hoped to add fuel to the fires of discord. By allowing England full play in settling the Belgian question Nicolas foresaw that her interests would be brought into conflict with those of France in a problem which touched both parties to the quick. This policy was always present in dealing with those questions in which Russia's direct interests were negligible. The question rises, what was Russia's purpose in carrying on this diplomatic play? Did she intend to ally herself with England or France? In 1838 there were no signs of this. Was Nesselrode satisfied with the artist's pleasure at a difficult assignment skillfully accomplished? Or was Russia convinced that the French alliance would never be of avail to her in a direct dispute with England? This last alternative seems to be the most reasonable answer to the puzzle. Russia did not disdain French assistance in defeating some of England's more objectionable projects, such as the constitution for Greece and the conference of the Powers on the Eastern Question. But she was unwilling to go beyond this negative cooperation with a "shady" government like that of Louis Philippe. That feeling of absolutist continuity in the government of Russia made Nicolas willing to wait for eighteen years to have his chance to say, in 1848, "I told you so." French support was good enough to disrupt Palmerston's pet scheme of a European conference which might have destroyed Russia's liberty of action in the Straits. It was not good enough to induce him to advance further, along the line urged by Medem and Pozzo di Borgo.

V

The Conference Plan in 1838

During the 1830's the project for a European conference on the Eastern Question was raised time and again. Its supporters could refer to the work of the Belgian conference in preventing war between the greater Powers over a problem which they all had very much at heart. The Greek conference of the three protecting Powers was functioning, if indifferently. In 1833 Metternich for a time had welcomed the idea of a conference on the Turko-Egyptian question, in order to subject Russia's protectorate in Turkey to the control of all the Powers. Ultimately he had been content with the degree of supervision over Russian policy in the Near East which was secured by the Münchengrätz convention.[1]

In 1838 a fresh incentive to call a conference on this question was furnished by the seeming unanimity of the Powers in rejecting Mohamed Ali's demand for sovereignty. The Powers agreed in threatening the Pasha of Egypt and in supporting the rights of the Sultan. What could be simpler than to bring together their representatives, to decide on a course of action which should remove the menace now looming up in the East? A conference would best convince Mohamed Ali that Europe's ranks were united. If, on the other hand, the Powers were not united, if they were afraid

[1] Ste. Aulaire, *op. cit.*, pp. 60-64.

to come together and decide on a common course of action, was there anything, in the long run, to hinder the Viceroy from gaining his independence? This was the question which haunted Mohamed Ali. At the same time, he had some hopes that for the sake of preserving the general peace the Powers would agree to arrange a settlement between him and his sovereign and to give their guarantee to it. In March 1838, when the Russian consul demanded that he disarm, Mohamed Ali replied that he could not disarm because he had no guarantee against an attack by the Sultan or against being deprived, through his sovereign's caprice, of all or some of his territories. The Powers should furnish him such a guarantee by underwriting the settlement of Kutaya and by granting him his independence, or, at least, the succession of all his territories.[2] The expression "guarantees" was continually on the Pasha's tongue at this time. But guarantees could be given only by the concert of the Powers, acting collectively.

The importance attached by the Pasha to collective steps, as well as his constant reference to guarantees, led Nesselrode to define the Russian viewpoint in identical despatches to London and Paris.[3] He included in them this despatch from Alexandria and his own despatch of March 1/13, in which he admonished the Pasha to be content with his present status and took solemn note of his promise not to commit any act

[2] R. A., A. Medem to Nesselrode, réservée, 20 March/1 April, 1838, folio 1, No. 4.

[3] R. A., Nesselrode to Pozzo di Borgo and Pahlen, confidentielle, 10/22 and 14/26 May 1838, folio 131, No. 1334, and folio 170, No. 1364.

of aggression. Nesselrode urged unanimity of language at Alexandria, on the part of all the Powers, to convince the Pasha that there was no divergence of views or interests among the chief governments of Europe. This was the limit to which Russia was willing to go in arranging unanimous, but not collective, steps at Alexandria. "It could not suit us to make of this question the object of a formal deliberation; for we always have a direct interest in avoiding anything that could cause to germinate in Paris or in London the idea of a common intervention in the affairs of the Orient. That is why the term of guarantee, which we find in Count Medem's despatch, by no means agrees with the views of our cabinet. Until now no allusion to such a guarantee has been made on the part of the maritime Powers. In any case we should decline such a combination if it happened to be presented. I was unwilling to leave Your Excellency in ignorance of our point of view on this subject, in order to point out to you in advance the language you should use if ideas, analogous to those mentioned in Count Medem's report happened to spring from the mind of the English [French] Ministry."

At the same time Nesselrode reminded Tatishchev at Vienna that "in this circumstance, as in every other, we count with full confidence on the unanimity of efforts which will be used by the agents of the two Imperial Courts to prevent the Viceroy from embarking on extreme measures." The original conclusion of his despatch to Vienna was crossed out. It reads: "There is no doubt but that he [Mohamed Ali] constantly nourishes the hope that the jealousy and

disunion of the Great Powers will turn to his own advantage.   In order to discourage this hope, it is indispensable to repeat to him constantly that the cabinets of Europe are unanimous in wishing one single.
. . ."   Nesselrode rejected the idea which he had
begun to express.   Evidently, he feared to give Metternich some hint which might be seized upon to open
the way for a collective deliberation.   He may have
had a premonition that Metternich would not be loath
to organize that conference which Russia could not
accept.[4]

But if Nesselrode had more than a glimmering of
the danger of a conference, his premonition was confirmed by the French reaction to the news of Mohamed
Ali's determination to declare his independence.   Louis
Philippe at once urged on the Russian chargé d'affaires,
already steeled against this suggestion by Nesselrode's
despatch, the importance of persuading both the Pasha
and the Sultan to allow the Powers to arrange their
difficulties.   The King did not mention the dangerous
word "conference," but he offered to join in any collective step which the Powers might decide to make
towards Mohamed Ali, in a purpose of conciliation
and peace.[5]   Plainly, the idea of a conference was
taking form in Louis Philippe's mind, for collective
steps could be arranged best of all by a conference or
"centre of entente."

Simultaneously, the idea of holding a conference on

[4] R. A., Nesselrode to Tatishchev, to Vienna, 11/23 May, 1838,
folio 218, No. 1346.

[5] R. A., Medem to Nesselrode, particulière, Paris, May 25/June
6, 1838, folio 169.

the Eastern Question was taking form in London. For
Louis Philippe its purpose would be to prevent hostilities from breaking out between the Pasha and the
Sultan, and to secure a peaceful solution, satisfactory
to the interests of the ruler of Egypt. Palmerston
had far wider purposes in mind. As he wrote to Paris
on June 8, 1838,[6] the Powers must prevent hostilities
between the Pasha and the Sultan, in order to prevent
Russia from seizing the Straits. England and France
should make a naval demonstration against Alexandria.
Separate declarations to Mohamed Ali had the advantage of speed; a joint and collective declaration,
however, would give England some hold over Russia,
if it were founded upon a previous and recorded agreement between the five Powers, giving to the five some
determining authority over the conduct of each. Since
this would be difficult to arrange, Palmerston favored
"a short convention between England and France on
the one hand, and Turkey on the other, by which the
two former should bind themselves for a limited time
to afford to the latter naval assistance in the event
of her demanding it to protect her territory against
attack; and the wording might be so framed as to
include the case either of Russia or of Mohamed Ali."
This would obviate the danger of a combination between Russia and France. Palmerston's optimum was
a conference to deprive Russia of her independence of
action; his second choice was a Franco-British alliance
with Turkey, to nullify Russia's power and influence
in the Levant.

[6] Bulwer, *op. cit.*, II, 269-271.

To the Austrian ambassador in London, Melbourne declared his readiness to agree with the other Powers.[7] According to Sabry,[8] the British ambassador in Vienna informed his government as early as June 19 (in Sabry, 1837: obviously a misprint for 1838) that Metternich authorized him to suggest that Austria, England, France, and Russia could agree in London on measures best suited to prevent Mohamed Ali from declaring his independence and on measures to be applied in case he made such a declaration. It must be noted that Metternich emphasized the measures to be taken against Mohamed Ali, and that he seemed to be justified in this by the unanimity of the Powers toward the Viceroy. Did he lose sight of Russia's attitude toward this attempt to limit her field of action in the Straits? Or was this oversight intentional?

Meanwhile, before he could have received this despatch from Sir Frederick Lamb, Palmerston had taken up the same subject with the Austrian ambassador in a conversation of June 24.[9] He urged on him the need for the Powers to agree in executing the threats which they had already made, unanimously but individually, against Mohamed Ali; English and French naval assistance would not be adequate at the beginning of the campaign; the Russians would probably send an army to aid the Sultan and to occupy the Dardanelles and Bosphorus; it was therefore useful to

[7] R. A., Medem to Nesselrode, Paris, 4/16 June, 1838, folio 169, No. 51, citing Esterhazy's letter to Apponyi.

[8] M. Sabry, *L'empire égyptien sous Mohamed Ali et la question d'Orient 1811-1849*, Paris, 1930; p. 416, no source cited.

[9] Sabry says May 24, obviously a misprint for June 24: *ibid.*, pp. 416-417.

agree by a previous concert among the four Powers on
the means of rendering military assistance to the Sultan; an English or French expedition would arouse
the jealousy of other Powers and speed up the advance
of the Russian troops; Austria was therefore desig-
nated to send a military expedition, since she could
do it, so Palmerston asserted, without arousing Russia's
jealousy.

The idea of using Austrian forces in the Levant was
very well suited to English interests, if not to Austrian ones. Austria would thereby be drawn away from
Russia and into alliance with England and France.
Russia would be isolated in Europe and in Turkey
deprived of any excuse for armed intervention. The
conference, which was to authorize the use of Austrian
troops, was doubly advantageous because it would bind
both Russia and France to follow the dictates of the
European concert, in which England could always
veto proposals unfavorable to her. This was particularly important for the London cabinet, for British
forces were scattered in Canada, Persia and Afghanistan, and a war with China was in the offing. At such
a time England could not expect to act in the Levant
with forces sufficient to maintain all her interests. It
was necessary for her, therefore, to defend the *status
quo*, which, at the moment, could be changed only to
her disadvantage. And the *status quo* could best be
maintained by submitting the entire Eastern Question
to collective deliberation and thus binding the action
of the two Powers which might harbor aggressive designs against the Ottoman Empire. Nothing could
please Palmerston more highly than the assurance that

Metternich would assist him in calling together a conference. At this time the Austrian chancellor was so optimistic of securing Russia's support for common action against Mohamed Ali that he even offered to France and England the cooperation of the Russian fleet in the Mediterranean. " 'Austria,' said the Prince Chancellor to me, 'would also join her fleet to it [a demonstration against Mohamed Ali], if she had one, and Russia would not refuse either, if her vessels were still in the Mediterranean.' " [10]

On June 29 the Russian agent in Vienna learned of these intrigues of Metternich with the English. "Metternich has formally authorized Lamb [the English ambassador] to propose to Palmerston to establish an entente, which would have its seat in London and which would decide on the measures best calculated to intimidate Mohamed Ali, as well as those which would have to be adopted if he should declare his independence. À propos of this, the Chancellor observes to Palmerston that his coming interview with the Emperor [Nicolas] would be favorable for overtures of all kinds; he also insists that the English ambassador should go in person to Toeplitz. In this regard, Sir F. Lamb has requested his government's commands." [11] Such was the unpleasant news that greeted Nesselrode at Carlsbad. Metternich's calculation was obvious. He was obviously not sorry to see Russia unable to undertake an aggression in Turkey, for

[10] R. A., Struve to Tatishchev, particulière, Vienna, June 21/July 3, 1838, folio 217.

[11] R. A., Struve to Nesselrode, chiffrée, Vienna, 17/29 June, 1838, folio 217.

Austria, handicapped by her uneasy Italians and
Magyars and by her rôle of watch-dog in the German
Confederation, was not able to muster an equal display
of force in case of action in the Ottoman Empire. All
these considerations led Palmerston to impart to the
other Powers his project for a conference, at the beginning of July.

On July 6 Palmerston wrote to Granville, in Paris,
urging Molé to join in organizing a conference in
London. If Mohamed Ali disturbed the peace, war
would follow between Russia on the one hand and
England and France on the other. Mohamed Ali
must be prevented from taking any dangerous step;
but if he should take it, a way had to be found to avert
the evil consequences which it might produce. A
previous concert among the five governments was the
best way out. "We wish, and so does Sébastiani, that
the representatives of the five Powers should be assembled in London; that we should there lay the case
before them, and propose a combined system of action;
that suggesting that if the Porte should want aid by
sea and by land, the three maritime Powers should give
aid by sea and Austria assistance by land; we should
state without disguise that the solitary interference of
Russia, however she may think herself justified or
bound to exert it, would excite great jealousy in this
part of the world; and that as in the general interest
and harmony it seems desirable to avoid such jealousy
with honor to all parties, and without any sacrifice
of important interests, we propose the military action
of Austria, which, from the intimate union existing
between Austria and Russia, would be perfectly com-

patible with the honor of Russia; while on the other hand, from the geographical position of Austria, it would not be the source of the same jealousy to England and France." [12]   This letter gives the maximum of Palmerston's aims. They were to set aside the treaty of Unkiar Iskelessi, to bind Russian action by joining the Russian fleet to those of France and England, and to separate Austria from Russia, by engaging the former to act in Turkey instead of the latter. The Russian government seems to have first learned in Paris of the plan to send the Russian fleet to join the French and English ones in the Levant.[13] The plan for Austrian military assistance was described shortly after by Molé himself as impracticable.[14] After Metternich had talked with the Russians at Toeplitz, he became quite indignant about Palmerston's proposal. He called it "a monstrous idea." In a letter of August 2 to Nesselrode, he wrote ironically: "If Lord Palmerston believes that Syria is a province adjacent to Austria, he still had, doubtless, as an excuse the well-known ignorance of the alleged statesmen who sometimes are found in charge of affairs of state in England." [15]   This irony overshoots its mark; Palmerston could not be justly accused of not knowing his geography. Metternich plainly intended to destroy Nesselrode's lingering suspicion that he

[12] Bulwer, *op. cit.*, II, 270-271.

[13] R. A., Medem to Nesselrode, Paris, 3/15 July, 1838, folio 169, No. 60.

[14] R. A., Medem to Nesselrode, Paris, 8/20 July, 1838, folio 169, No. 62.

[15] F. F. Martens, *Recueil, etc.*, IV, pt. 1, 478-479.

himself might be the real author of the plan for an Austrian expedition to Syria.

During these preliminary negotiations with Austria and France, Palmerston had avoided discussing with the Russian ambassador future contingencies of the Eastern Question.[16] But on July 6, the day on which Palmerston wrote to Paris definitely announcing his intention of summoning a European conference, he gave Pozzo di Borgo the first intimation of his project. "Having asked Lord Palmerston if he had taken any step in regard to the Pasha of Egypt to dissuade him from declaring himself independent, he replied that the instructions given to the British consul order him to act in this sense. He added that he intended to come to an agreement with France in order to propose a common entente of the five Powers on eastern affairs. I did not say a single word more, because I should not run the risk of entering into a discussion of this question. This is Louis Philippe's dominating idea, which we have had to thrust aside. I judged, however, that I should not leave Your Excellency in ignorance of this particular. On my asking what were the motives for the presence of the English squadron at Toulon, Lord Palmerston said to me that it was a mere visit and military promenade. There must be communications passing between the two courts. It seems to me more prudent to await for their nature to be disclosed, rather than to question them, without, however, diminishing our watch over the material means which they might increase. For the mo-

[16] R. A., Pozzo di Borgo to Nesselrode, London, June 21/July 3, 1838, folio 129, No. 53.

ment no preparations are being made in the ports." [17]

Palmerston was not alone in his idea of organizing a concert of the Powers. The French premier wished to establish his own conference in Paris. "He [Molé] intends to assemble the representatives of the Great Powers in order to submit to them the proposal to make, on a certain day, towards Mohamed Ali, a simultaneous and identical step which would prove the perfect accord existing among the cabinets and henceforth would leave him no doubt as to the unanimous opposition which his plans of independence would meet. Lord Palmerston has let it be known here that he also was going to propose to the ambassadors of Russia and Austria to join him in coming to an agreement regarding this simultaneous declaration, the importance and utility of which had already been recognized by the cabinets of London and Paris." [18]   By the middle of July, however, Lord Palmerston relaxed considerably his striving to summon a conference on eastern affairs. Palmerston now appeared to adopt Molé's original opinion that separate, but identical, steps would suffice to restrain Mohamed Ali. Molé showed some pique at Palmerston's adopting his own idea of simultaneous, but not collective, steps without crediting him with the authorship. In some irritation he reminded Louis Philippe that it was as a result of his own objections that Palmerston had abandoned his first idea of common and collective action.[19]

17 R. A., Pozzo di Borgo to Nesselrode, chiffrée, London, June 24/July 6, 1838, folio 129.

18 R. A., Medem to Nesselrode, Paris, 3/15 July, 1838, folio 169, No. 60.

19 *Revue rétrospective*, p. 100.

But in the beginning of August, the conference idea was abruptly revived by Lord Palmerston. He was now aroused to fresh action by the Russian declaration, despatched from Toeplitz to the French and English cabinets. Russia proposed that the Powers issue simultaneous and identical declarations to the Pasha of Egypt, in order to restrain him within the bounds of duty to his sovereign. Nicolas invited England and France to use their naval forces against Mohamed Ali. He threatened, if appealed to by the Porte in distress, to come to its assistance as required by the treaty of Unkiar Iskelessi. This declaration was received with calm and even sympathy by Count Molé. In London, however, it arrived like a bombshell. The statement for London was delivered to Palmerston on August 5. "He [Palmerston] appeared satisfied with its contents; however, on reaching the passage regarding the case in which Russia would be obliged to interfere with force to help the Sultan, he stopped and said that in that case alarm would be general in Europe. I refrained from entering into any discussion, observing to him that our common efforts tended to avoid that, a truth which he concurred in. Lord Melbourne, without referring to the case of war, believes England should take measures such as to prevent the Pasha from declaring himself independent. Prince Metternich orders Prince Esterhazy to consider my instructions as if they were addressed to him." [20]

[20] R. A., Pozzo di Borgo to Nesselrode, London, July 29/August 10, 1838, folio 129, No. 76.

The Russian declaration stirred Palmerston to new activity. He at once resolved to establish a concert of the Powers in London. He invited each of the ambassadors of the four Great Powers to call on him at the same hour, without warning the representatives of Austria, Russia, and Prussia that they would meet all together. They learned of this stratagem by accident. Pozzo di Borgo then hesitated to go, but decided to attend after Esterhazy offered to enter first at Downing Street. The Austrian representative promised to warn Palmerston not to cause a divergence among the Powers, since none had arisen so far and the display of divergence would only encourage the Pasha to defy the Powers. When the four ambassadors were assembled, Palmerston proposed that the five Powers establish a concert as to their future course in case Mohamed Ali persisted in executing his project of independence. Sébastiani declared that he had instructions to deliberate on Palmerston's proposal and that an attack on the *status quo* of the Ottoman Empire would be the signal for war. Esterhazy and Bülow said they would write to their cabinets; Pozzo di Borgo did not utter a single word, and the meeting broke up without leaving any formal record.[21] Molé read to the Russian chargé in Paris Sébastiani's account of this strange attempt to establish a conference by surprise. "Sébastiani's despatch says in very clear terms that the Principal Secretary of State [Palmerston] had been justly terrified by this announcement of the sending

[21] R. A., Pozzo di Borgo to Nesselrode, London, 3/15 August, 1838, folio 129, No. 77.

of a Russian army corps to Asia Minor, that he recognized the importance of confirming even better Russia's ambitious views and, in order not to leave Count Pozzo di Borgo any chance to concert with the representatives of Austria and Prussia regarding the explanations to be given, he had concealed from all of them the purpose of the meeting, having taken only Sébastiani into his confidence." [22]

Pozzo di Borgo's indignation at this diplomatic ruse knew no bounds. "I may dispense, Monsieur le Comte, with commentaries on the conduct of this minister. He exercises his talent in arousing difficulties in a capricious manner and in perverting the best of intentions. This is the first idea aroused in him by the Emperor's frank and loyal explanations. We shall see how he will reply in writing, in the answer which he has said he is preparing." [23] The mild and conciliatory Melbourne expressed to Pozzo di Borgo his disapproval of Palmerston's attempt to open a conference by surprise. But even he pointed out that Russia's intention to execute a treaty against which England had protested merited the serious consideration of the cabinet. To Esterhazy, the Austrian ambassador, Melbourne spoke out more strongly in condemnation of Palmerston's manner of action. The Austrian ambassador promised his Russian colleague that he would decline a conference and in case the ambassadors were again summoned, he

[22] R. A., Medem to Nesselrode, réservée, Paris, 10/22 August, 1838, folio 170, No. 70.

[23] R. A., Pozzo di Borgo to Nesselrode, London, 3/15 August, 1838, folio 129, No. 77.

would speak first, to destroy Palmerston's illusions of separating Russia and Austria.[24]

Palmerston's written reply to the Russian declaration of Toeplitz was a new brief in favor of a conference. He ignored the Russian suggestions for settling the Egyptian question. Instead he proposed to establish a concert of the five Powers on the measures to be adopted in case Mohamed Ali threw off his allegiance to the Porte. He asked Pozzo di Borgo to request his court for instructions to take part in its deliberation. The Russian ambassador in London was greatly anguished by this proposal. He still regarded Louis Philippe as the original author of the suggestion, and felt that Palmerston, with the aid of Sébastiani wished to make himself the dictator of the conference. "*All eastern policy*, Monsieur le Comte, *is comprised in this project*. Its first effect, if it were adopted, would be to deprive Russia of all the advantages of her special position. The great system, begun two centuries ago, consolidated by the succession of so many victories and so much wisdom, would be subjected to the malignant inquisition of the British minister, aided and backed by the complicity and support of the Tuileries cabinet. The treaties existing between Russia and the Porte would be virtually abolished or paralyzed, because, when the Emperor should decide to apply them, England and France would bring to the conference their objections and protests. . . . This labyrinth would have no way out, Monsieur le Comte. We should have to break through it and then

[24] R. A., Pozzo di Borgo to Nesselrode, London, 11/23 August, 1838, folio 129, No. 79.

we should have a point of departure very different
from that in which we are happily placed." Pozzo di
Borgo urged his government to make only a verbal
reply, or even to declare that Palmerston's note would
be regarded as "non avenue." [25]

Meanwhile, Nesselrode had begun counter-measures
against Palmerston's proposal. While attending the
coronation of the Austrian Emperor as King of
Lombardy, he was able to win over Metternich completely to Russia's view of the conference proposal.
This was probably easier since Metternich expected
some agitation to arise in France against the manœuvre
arranged between himself and the Holy See, to force
the French to evacuate Ancona. Nesselrode reported
to the Emperor from Milan on September 4, 1838:
". . . Your Majesty, I make bold to believe, will deign
to honor with His entire approbation the attitude which
Count Pozzo di Borgo has taken in declining peremp-
torily the attempt made by Lord Palmerston for the
purpose of drawing the representatives of the other
courts to set up a special conference at London on
eastern affairs." Metternich had promised to send
more precise instructions to Esterhazy in London; he
was to refuse to accept any proposal for making London
the centre of a common deliberation on Egyptian affairs.
Metternich added: "That since all the Powers were
in complete accord on the necessity for maintaining
the *status quo* in the east, there was nothing to discuss
or to deliberate on in London; that a conference of

[25] R. A., Pozzo di Borgo to Nesselrode, London, 26 August/7 September, 1838, folio 129, No. 83.

the five Powers, so far from strengthening their union, could, on the contrary, only contribute to create difficulties and divergences of opinion, by which Mohamed Ali would be the first to profit for the benefit of his ambition; that, in this conviction, Prince Esterhazy would receive express instructions positively to refuse his cooperation in any collective deliberation in London on the Eastern Question, if Lord Palmerston happened to renew that proposal." [26]

Palmerston's note proposing a conference and Pozzo di Borgo's new cry of alarm were received by Nesselrode in Berlin. Nicolas wrote out his directions on the despatch from London: "You will confine yourself to saying that our reply has preceded the question; that it is contained in our despatch [from Toeplitz] . . . and that I shall not add *a single word*." [27]

Nesselrode's calm note to the Emperor on the following day may have been calculated to counteract the inflammatory effect of Pozzo di Borgo's despatches on the Emperor's irritable temper. He wrote: "The English cabinet persists in its intention of making of the Egyptian question the object of a collective deliberation, and Lord Palmerston has made this formal proposal in a letter addressed to Count Pozzo di Borgo." Nicolas summoned up his feeling on the matter: "It is pitiful: the reply to Palmerston is easy, it is an *exhausted* subject; the same is true in my opinion of the interminable Dutch affair, in which we

[26] R. A., Nesselrode to Emperor, Milan, 23 August/4 September, 1838, *Rapports à l'Empereur,* folio 66, pp. 332-334.

[27] Emperor's note on despatch, received in Berlin, 4/16 September, 1838.

have long ago said everything." [28]   Accordingly Nesselrode sent a private letter to Pozzo di Borgo, on September 21, from Berlin.   "The crisis is over and the accord of the Great Powers is complete.   Why therefore provoke a deliberation on mere eventualities?" [29]

On October 3, 1838, Nesselrode replied from Berlin to Palmerston's note.   He declared that there was no necessity and no utility in summoning a conference, and that Russia, therefore, maintained the view expressed in her Toeplitz despatch.   On October 9 the Russian ambassador read this to Palmerston, and then allowed him to run through it for himself.   He was careful not to leave him a copy, in order that Palmerston might not publish it among parliamentary papers and thus accuse Russia of refusing European conciliation in the Eastern Question.   "After running through it twice and very attentively, Lord Palmerston said that it set aside the principal point, which was the purpose of his note: namely, to prevent each Power from acting in isolation if events made action necessary; that this object having failed, uncertainty continued and consequently suspicions and apprehensions. . . .   Lord Palmerston replied that thus the Emperor [of Russia] remained his own master, to act according to his own will, and that, if circumstances arose, England would not fail to intervene even at the risk of bringing on war. . . ." [30]   Palmerston ended

---

[28] R. A., Nesselrode to Emperor and Emperor to Nesselrode, *Rapports à l'Empereur,* Berlin, 5/17 September, 1838, folio 66, pp. 330-331.

[29] F. F. Martens, *Recueil, etc.,* XII, 73.

[30] R. A., Pozzo di Borgo to Nesselrode, London, 30 September/12 October, 1838, folio 130, No. 91.

by promising a detailed reply to the Russian note. The threat of war contained in this oral reply was a vital factor in urging the Russian cabinet to make haste in sending to London its despatch of November 1, justifying its actions in Persia. Nesselrode was anxious to weaken England's motives for rushing headlong into a war in defense of her interests, which seemed to be threatened by Russia throughout the east.

Meanwhile, Russia took care to secure from the French cabinet a restatement of its unwillingness to enter a conference in London on eastern affairs. Molé declared to the recently returned Russian ambassador, Count Pahlen, that he knew nothing of Palmerston's proposal to Russia to establish a collective deliberation at London and agreed that in a matter of such major interest for Russia, the Emperor could not allow deliberations to be organized by Palmerston and in London. After learning of the Prussian and Austrian refusals to participate in such a conference, Molé was even more explicit in his disapproval of Palmerston's initiative.[31]

Palmerston's new note was a long harangue against Russia. He revived all the old causes of conflict between the two Powers. He accused Russia of instigating Persia to menace the Indian frontier by her alliance with the Afghan chiefs. He indicted Russia for her alleged desire to exterminate the Circassians, struggling for their independence. He refurbished the English grievance against the Unkiar Iskelessi treaty. He suspected Russia of nefarious projects in maintain-

[31] R. A., Pahlen to Nesselrode, Paris, 18/30 October, 1838, folio 170, No. 87.

ing in perpetual readiness in the Baltic a war fleet of
thirty vessels. He closed this long hymn of hate by
declaring that what he had said was the result of four
cabinet meetings held on this question and that the
ministry would act accordingly. Pozzo di Borgo re-
viewed the strong and weak points of the Russian
position. Austria seemed to be moving towards an
entente with England. France could throw decisive
forces into action. "The culminating point of the dispute is Constantinople. If the Sultan wishes to go over
to our enemies in a manner which may render our
resentment necessary, the principal struggle will take
place in these regions and on this territory. This
eventual case has formed the object of the meditations
of the Imperial cabinet for so long, that I could not
permit myself the slightest observation. In examining
the forces which our adversaries could immediately em-
ploy against us, to violate the peace, there are none at
their disposal for the moment, which would be capable
of executing any essential enterprise; they would serve
only to authorize us to set our own forces in movement
with all the premises of a definitive success. It is true
that the English fleet in the Mediterranean will be increased to twelve ships-of-the-line with others of less
size and the armed steamboats, but it is not to be pre-
sumed that they would wish to break the peace with
such limited means and that the Sultan would be willing
to turn over to them the Dardanelles and Bosphorus,
without having any other protection against the consequences. France herself would not join such an
enterprise in the present state of her armaments and
it would be fortunate for her to meditate in the in-

terval on the misfortunes which a servile conduct towards England and hostility to Russia would not fail to bring on Europe and on herself." [32]

This despatch had been awaited with anxiety in St. Petersburg. With tension so strong over Persia and Turkey, the Russian cabinet was prepared for the worst. Nesselrode at once sent the London despatches to the Emperor. His accompanying note breathes an almost audible sigh of relief. "I admit to Your Majesty that I cannot consider the circumstances so grave as our Ambassador has depicted them. I expected a long series of fresh accusations and determinations taken against us. Instead, I find . . . only a repetition of a few old grievances, so often refuted, and reproaches so absurd that, in my eyes, it would be impossible for England to base on them alone a system of open attack on Russia. Far from that, I still do not find any indication presaging a rupture between the two countries. It is scarcely possible on England's part in the situation which she herself is in. It appears on the contrary that she fears us at all the points at which she feels herself vulnerable, and, in order to defeat the designs which she persists in attributing to us, she seeks to create enemies for us everywhere and tries to lead us into trouble with our most intimate allies. It is evidently for this purpose that Lord Melbourne communicated to Count Pozzo di Borgo the copy of a rather singular note which Prince Metternich is supposed to have written to Sir Fred. Lamb. . . ." [33]   To this

[32] R. A., Pozzo di Borgo to Nesselrode, London, 11/23 October, 1838, folio 130, No. 93.

[33] R. A., Nesselrode to Emperor, 23 October, 1838, o.s., folio 66. pp. 291-292, *Rapports à l'Empereur*.

exposition of Nesselrode's view of matters, Nicolas replied somewhat crisply: "I share your view entirely, but let us be prudent both in Constantinople and in Vienna." Two days before receiving these reports from London, Nicolas had written to his "father-commander," Paskievich, Prince of Warsaw, one of the greatest military and political authorities of the Empire: "Granted their [the English] attitude, there is no guaranteeing but that the bomb may explode from one day to the next, and that they may not commit some act of intolerable audacity. There is one obstacle in their way, the lack of troops; but for that they undoubtedly will push others forward, maybe, the French; although I do not believe that the calculating Louis Philippe would swallow this trick, for where should he send his troops when he himself is barely holding on. Anyway, whatever happens, we are ready; I will certainly not cheat anyone, but I will not allow anyone to cheat me; just let them try. . . ." [34]

During 1838 two more notes were exchanged between London and Petersburg on the desirability of a conference. The seemingly endless bickering was closed in December by Nesselrode's declaration that he was satisfied with Palmerston's reception of his latest note; Palmerston himself appeared convinced of the uselessness of a conference regarding possibilities which now seemed far removed, since all the Powers were unanimous in wishing to see the peace of the Levant maintained.[35]   And here the idea of the conference was

[34] Shcherbatov, *op. cit.,* V, 372-373.

[35] R. A., Nesselrode to Ribeaupierre, Nesselrode to Tatishchev, to Berlin and Vienna, 20 December and 22 December, 1838, o.s., folio 38, No. 1491, and folio 218, No. 1511.

dropped by both parties to the dispute, until the events
of 1839 led to its revival in more persistent, and, for
Russia, more dangerous form.

But the threat of war between Russia and England
had been caught up by the lesser Powers of Europe.
At Copenhagen the conflict was regarded as inevitable
and the King of Denmark ordered his minister at Vienna to ask Metternich what attitude he should then
adopt. The Swedish minister approached the Austrian
chancellor with a similar query. Metternich tried to
persuade them that no crisis was imminent and urged
them to refrain from any premature steps.[36] Even
the Hospodar of Valachia, who found it hard to please
both his masters, Turkey and Russia, was supposed to
have abandoned Bucharest for Vienna rather suddenly,
in fear that the Russians would cross the Pruth and
occupy his territories on their way to Constantinople,
to drive the English fleet from the Dardanelles.[37]
Metternich's own view was that neither England nor
Russia was anxious to engage in serious warfare in
Turkey or in Persia. Nicolas would not pick up the
glove thrown down by England, but if he did resist,
England would withdraw.[38] The French ambassador
in Vienna was certain that Metternich wished to avoid
a war, but if it came, he would gradually turn against
Russia.[39]

[36] R. A., Struve to Nesselrode, Vienna, 28 October/9 November,
1838, chiffrée, folio 217, No. 77.

[37] R. A., Ste. Aulaire to Barante, Vienna, 20 November, 1838,
deciphered by Russian and Austrian secret service; in folio 217, No.
96, secrète.

[38] Metternich, *Mémoires, documents et écrits divers laissé par le
Prince de,* 8 vols., Paris, 1880-84. VI, 289.   ,

[39] R. A., folio 217, No. 96, secrète.

While the secondary states of Europe were anxiously scanning the political horizon, the English cabinet was examining its first line of attack and defense, the navy. During November, 1838, the Melbourne government resolved on a considerable strengthening of its squadrons. As an alternative, or possibly, as a justifying pretext, Palmerston proposed to ask Russia not to equip more than a certain portion of her fleet the following spring.[40] When this proposal was made in January, 1839, it was rejected by the Russian government, and the increase in the English fleet was carried through.

The naval competition of these two world Powers was but an index to the tenseness of the struggle going on between them throughout Asia. From September to December, 1838, their relations were put to a severe strain over the Perso-Afghan question. The conciliatory Russian explanations of November 1, 1838, contributed to relax the tension, and Melbourne at least urged the necessity for coming to an entente with Russia on Middle Asiatic affairs. When the news was received in London late in December that the Afghan expedition had been decided upon and, according to schedule, must be on its way, the London cabinet could rest assured that its prestige, badly threatened in July, would be restored by the most effective means. It was also relieved to learn that the expedition against Persia, urged by McNeill, had been abandoned. This meant that the danger of an armed struggle between Russia and England on Persian territory had been avoided.

[40] Lord Broughton, *Recollections of a Long Life,* 6 vols., London, 1909-11, V, 168-169.

The clearing up of the Asiatic situation could thus contribute, as it did during the spring and summer of 1839, to allay, not mutual suspicion, but at least the fear of an immediate collision in the heart of Asia.

During 1838 Russia had once again resisted with success the attempts made by Austria, France and England to set up a European conference on the Eastern Question. Nicolas had maintained that freedom of diplomatic and military action which was essential if Russia was to be able, at the critical moment, to seize and hold the Straits. But that "elbow-room" might be lost. It would vanish from the very moment when Turkey refused to fulfil the obligations of Unkiar Iskelessi. The sharp diplomatic offensive which Palmerston was carrying on in Europe, through the conference plan, was paralleled by Ponsonby's strenuous efforts to wrench the Sublime Porte from Russia's tutelage.

VI

ANGLO-RUSSIAN RIVALRY FOR INFLUENCE IN TURKEY

THE centre of the Anglo-Russian struggle was transferred by August, 1838, from London to Constantinople. Palmerston's efforts to establish a conference
on the Eastern Question were, to be sure, continued.
They promised to create diplomatic embarrassments
for Russia. But the real seat of rivalry was Constantinople. Meanwhile, the European side of the question—
the Straits—had overshadowed its Egyptian side—the
problem of the relation of the Pasha of Egypt to the
Sultan. Without renouncing his ultimate aim, the
erection of an independent state, Mohamed Ali seemed
unlikely to embark on any immediate steps. His journey to the Senaar, to inspect alleged gold mines in that
province, gave a respite in the Egyptian problem from
October, 1838, till March, 1839. But the European
side of the difficulty remained. The great question
was, could England destroy Russia's preponderance in
Turkey and thus make the treaty of Unkiar Iskelessi
a dead letter? In Constantinople Lord Ponsonby, in
a characteristic spasm of impetuous activity, set himself to the task of establishing his exclusive influence
over the councils of the Porte.

The sudden increase of English interest in Turkey
made itself felt in July, 1838. On receiving from
Teheran the news that McNeill had been compelled to
break with the Shah because the latter, evidently sup-

ported by Russia, persisted in a policy contrary to English interests, Lord Ponsonby at once set about establishing an Anglo-Turk entente, which was to nullify the Russo-Turk alliance. This change was not at first noticed by the Russian chargé d'affaires, but it soon aroused the attention and the indignation of the French ambassador, Admiral Roussin.[1] Three immediate aims were pursued by the British representatives in Constantinople, and they were achieved almost before the representatives of the other Powers were aware of the great modification which was being effected in Turkish policy. One of these aims was to send Reshid Pasha, the Turkish foreign minister, on an extraordinary mission to Europe. In the beginning, this plan seems to have been connected with Palmerston's attempt to organize a conference on the Eastern Question. Once in London, Reshid might point out to the Powers that he was there to settle the Egyptian question and invite their cooperation. In any case, Reshid's presence in London would be a guarantee of close accord between England and Turkey and might render the Russo-Turkish treaty of 1833 void in fact. A second aim was, by taking advantage of the Sultan's hatred for Mohamed Ali, to secure commercial concessions favorable to English trade. This result was achieved within a few weeks. A third aim was to join the Turkish fleet to the English squadron for a cruise, by encouraging the Sultan to hope that the two fleets would be used against the Pasha of Egypt. The roots of the new Anglo-Turk entente lay in the dissatisfac-

[1] *Revue rétrospective*, p. 103.

tion of the Sultan with the conditions established by
the convention of Kutaya in 1833.   Desire for revenge
burned fiercely in him.   Even if Mohamed Ali had regarded the 1833 agreement as permanent, the Sultan
would have been eager to seize the first opportunity
to recover the territories which he had yielded to the
superior force of his vassal. The policy of the European
Powers in the summer of 1838 was directed towards
maintaining the agreement of Kutaya and restraining
the Pasha from violation of it.   The Porte appreciated
this service, rendered to it in its helplessness by the
European governments, but it could not be satisfied with
this negative support.   The Sultan wanted to bring
the Powers to assist him actively in his struggle to reduce the territorial possessions of Mohamed Ali and
to compel him to diminish his armaments.   If Egypt
and Syria suffered because of the excessive armaments
of the Pasha, the provinces of the Sultan were groan-
ing no less loudly.   So long as the *status quo* was continued, there could be no relief for either party to the
dispute.   The Porte let the Russian chargé clearly
feel the inadequacy of the defensive support given to
it during the 1838 crisis.   "While making himself the
organ of the gratitude of the Porte for the continued
interest of the Powers in its favor, Reshid Pasha observed that their language displayed once more the
intention of making the *status quo* last indefinitely,
while the security of the Sultan imperiously demanded
that an end be put to it." [2]

This unexpected belligerence of the Sultan was noted

[2] R. A., Rückmann to Divov, Constantinople, 16/28 August, 1838,
folio 49.

with equal disquiet by the French government. The Sultan seemed to abandon himself to ideas of revenge against Mohamed Ali; the Powers must repress the danger from this side, for it was just as great as from the side of Egypt.[3]

England and Turkey were united by a common desire to restrict or even destroy the rising power of Mohamed Ali. At the same time, they had another ground of common understanding. England was now at swords' points with Persia over the latter's persistence in the siege of Herat. Turkey was chronically in bad relations with her neighbor to the east. Religious differences and territorial quarrels had long divided them. In the beginning of July, 1838, their relations entered on a new period of crisis. The Persian princes, rivals for the throne of Shah Mohamed, had fled from Persia and now the Shah demanded that they be extradited to Persia. The Turkish government refused. The old quarrel over the border province of Muharemieh was revived at the same time by nomad raids.[4] At the end of July, 1838, Ponsonby received from McNeill despatches describing the state of crisis between Russia and England over Persia. He at once set to work to sweep the Porte off its feet. Within three weeks all the immediate aims set by England in her Turkish policy had been achieved. Reshid Pasha was already departing for his tour of the European capitals. Just before his departure the new Anglo-

[3] R. A., Molé to Sercey, to St. Petersburg, 26 September, 1838, deciphered by Austrian secret bureau; in folio 217, No. 97, secrète.

[4] R. A., Rückmann to Rodofinikin, Constantinople, 21 June/3 July, 1838, folio 94, No. 94.

Turkish treaty of commerce received its preliminary signature. And two days after Reshid had sailed for Trieste, the Porte announced officially that the Turkish fleet would join the English squadron under Lord Stopford, for a joint cruise in an unannounced direction. It was supposed that Ponsonby had even promised to secure a foreign loan for the Porte, but that the state of the empire was too precarious to tempt European bankers.[5]

In early August Reshid made his farewell call on the Russian chargé d'affaires. He tried to disarm the Russian suspicions of his purposes. "The Porte is well persuaded of the interest which the Powers take in its favor, and of their firm determination to compel the Pasha of Egypt to respect the *status quo*. But that is insufficient for the security of the Divan. Mohamed Ali, as is plain, is farther removed than ever from renouncing his ambitious hopes. The Sultan can never be at rest on that score. The constantly hostile attitude of his dangerous vassal obliges His Highness to bear sacrifices too onerous for the *status quo* to be of long duration. So painful a tension, and so permanent, on both sides, must inevitably, in the long run, lead to consequences absolutely contrary to the pacific views of the Great Powers. It is necessary for them to take counsel on some solution of these difficulties. The policy of Russia and of the courts of Vienna and Berlin rests on a solid and logical system. The Porte counts implicitly on their support. But that does not hold for the maritime Powers, whose conduct is subordinated to the fluctuations of parliamentary ma-

5 Bulwer, *op. cit.*, II, 272-273.

jorities and of public opinion. That is what has persuaded the Sultan to send me especially to Paris and
to London, to see what dispositions dominate there today, and to request the decisive cooperation of those
two governments." When pressed to be more concrete,
Reshid spoke of territorial retrocessions, of disarming
the Egyptian fleet, of discharging a part of the Pasha's
army. The Russian chargé pointed out that Mohamed
Ali would yield in such vital points only to force, and
that England and France would never act together if
action had to be taken against him. Reshid seemed
much annoyed at this blunt prediction. Roussin, the
French ambassador, was even louder in condemning
Reshid's mission, and warned the Porte against disturbing the *status quo*.[6]

The new treaty of commerce was negotiated in great
haste and secrecy and signed on August 16, 1838, just
before Reshid's departure. Ostensibly, he was to negotiate the several points which had been left unsettled
in the preliminary treaty. As early as February, 1838,
Palmerston had instructed Ponsonby to bring to the
attention of the Porte the great importance of one of
the chief features of the treaty under negotiation.[7]
That was the abolition of monopolies. Officially, the
capitulations between the Porte and the Powers gave
full liberty of commerce to Europeans in Turkey.
Actually, trade was made very difficult and less profit-
able because of the elaborate system of monopolies
which had grown up. Each governor was free to de-

---

[6] R. A., Rückmann to Nesselrode, Constantinople, 2/14 August,
1838, folio 48, No. 102.

[7] Hall, *op. cit.*, p. 231.

clare any commodity a monopoly.   Then it could be
sold by the peasant only to the government's agents,
at a fixed price, and the government later resold it at
a great profit to native and foreign merchants.   The
Turkish government had been negotiating for several
years with both France and England, but was loath to
suppress its countless monopolies, for it was one of the
chief sources of income for the officials of the Porte, if
not for the treasury itself.   In February, 1838, Palmerston pointed out a feature of the treaty, overlooked
till then.   The abolition of monopolies would destroy
the economic system built up by Mohamed Ali in Egypt
and to some extent in Syria and Arabia.   He was the
chief merchant of the country, and the peasants were
obliged to sell to his agents.   By abolishing monopolies
the Porte could accomplish two good deeds at once.
It would destroy the economic foundation for the superior prosperity of the Pasha of Egypt.   At the same
time, it would reassert, in a treaty signed with a Great
Power, its sovereign rights over Egypt and Syria, including the right to apply treaties to those nearly independent provinces.   In July, 1838, this argument
prevailed over the Sultan's fear of ruining his own
sources of revenue.   Bulwer asserts that the treaty of
August 16 was concluded without Palmerston's consent.[8]   In any case, the principle on which the treaty
was negotiated had been indicated months before by
Palmerston himself.   Another feature of the treaty was
that it increased the import duty by two percent and
the export duty by nine percent.   This monstrous
handicap for Turkish agriculture and industry very

8 Bulwer, *op. cit.,* II, 264.

nearly dealt a final blow to the prosperity of the empire. Bulwer asserts that it was the Turks who insisted on this feature, against his own persuasions.[9] Beyond a doubt, the Turks were extremely anxious to conclude the treaty. The political advantage which it seemed to offer blinded them to its economic consequences. But the Turks did refuse one concession which Ponsonby added to the list, when he saw how great was the Porte's eagerness. That was the right of free transit across Turkey. At the last minute Tahir Pasha saved the Porte from that unnecessary sacrifice.[10]

The negotiation was kept a secret until the signature had actually taken place. As late as August 14 Reshid Pasha assured the Russian representative that his frequent conversations with the English secretary, Bulwer, concerned only partial questions and would not affect the commercial treaties in force between the Porte and the other Powers.[11] The French ambassador was extremely indignant at the way in which his English colleague had negotiated this treaty, and publicly declared that France would never accept it. He accused England of disturbing the *status quo* in the Levant and of provoking Mohamed Ali to desperate measures. In early September, 1838, the French ministry joined its protests to those of its ambassador.[12] Molé com-

---

[9] Bulwer, *op. cit.*, II, 265.

[10] E. de Cadalvène et E. Barrault, *Deux années de l'histoire de l'Orient,* 2 vols., Paris, 1840, I, 348-354.

[11] R. A., Rückmann to Divov, Constantinople, 2/14 August, 1838, folio 48, No. 103.

[12] R. A., Pahlen to Nesselrode, Paris, chiffrée, 9/21 September, 1838, folio 170, No. 76.

plained bitterly to the English ambassador in Paris of the slight inflicted on the French government.[13]   Louis Philippe wished to adhere to the treaty, to secure its advantages for France, but only after expressly excluding it from affecting Syria and Egypt.   French commerce was much more bound up with Alexandria than with the Turkish provinces.[14]   By the end of September, Molé lowered his tone, and admitted that France would probably adhere to the treaty, since Palmerston insisted on its execution.[15]   But the slight rankled.

The Pasha of Egypt now put an end to the painful uncertainty of the Powers by announcing that he was ready to apply the treaty of August 16, 1838, to his territories.   As owner of nearly all the soil, it would be an easy matter for Mohamed Ali to make sure that the fellahin sold their product only to him; a little shifting of his economic apparatus and he was ready to carry on in the old way.   The Porte had dealt itself a terrible blow, while the Pasha escaped unscathed. The Porte continually postponed the execution of the treaty, and it was not until after the crisis was over, in 1841, that it began to be executed in part, and imperfectly in Turkey.   Mischef says that the Russian consul influenced the Pasha to accept the treaty, but quotes no source.[16]   Whoever or whatever was responsi-

[13] Hall, *op. cit.,* p. 234.

[14] R. A., Pahlen to Nesselrode, Paris, 21 September/3 October, 1838, folio 170, No. 81.

[15] R. A., Pahlen to Nesselrode, Paris, chiffrée, 14/26 September, 1838, folio 170, No. 77.

[16] P. H. Mischef, *La Mer Noire et les Détroits de Constantinople,* Paris, 1899, p. 321.

ble for this unexpected outcome, the path was now smoothed for French adherence to the treaty.[17]

But was this mysterious treaty only a treaty of commerce? Might it not contain some secret political clauses? Was it not a masked form by which Turkey had transferred her alliance from Russia to England? This rumor ran through Constantinople. It was repeated in Berlin.[18] In London Pozzo di Borgo raised a cry of alarm. This was just at the greatest heat of his controversy with Palmerston on Russian policy in Persia, on the Russian rejection of the conference on the Eastern Question, on Russia's refusal to limit the size of her fleet. Pozzo di Borgo seemed to expect a declaration of war from the English minister at every next encounter. On hearing of the August 16 treaty, he at once pictured it as an alliance between Turkey and England. The commercial treaty between England and Austria was also a sign that these two Powers were about to form a league against Russia. France was to be won over by Lord Holland, who had just been sent to Paris, to secure French assent to the new treaty with Turkey.[19] On this despatch Nicolas wrote in pencil: "We had to expect it; but the danger is in Constantinople, and there we must recommend all vigilance to Butenev, so that we may not be betrayed by the Porte." Pozzo di Borgo's next despatch was no less alarming, but Nesselrode was better steeled to

[17] R. A., Pahlen to Nesselrode, Paris, 30 September/12 October, 1838, folio 170, No. 83; Hall, *op. cit.*, p. 234.

[18] R. A., Ribeaupierre to Nesselrode, Berlin, 9/21 October, 1838, folio 38, No. 103.

[19] R. A., Pozzo di Borgo to Nesselrode, London, 30 September/12 October, 1838, folio 130, No. 91.

it. This time the Emperor's comment was: ". . . Let us be prudent both in Constantinople and in Vienna." [20]

The third aim of English policy was to effect the junction of the Turkish and English fleets. The Turkish ministers were reported to have hesitated, for fear of giving offense to Russia. But the Russian declaration of Toeplitz had announced that the Emperor welcomed any measures taken in the Mediterranean to curb the power of Mohamed Ali. The decision was then made, in favor of the joint cruise.[21] Russia was bound to be alarmed by this fraternizing of her supposed ally with her bitterest enemy. But France was also painfully affected by this innovation. "Count Molé did not conceal from me that the combined movements of the Turkish and English squadrons seem to him extraordinary, and he finds especially strange the measure which has resulted in placing an English officer on board each Ottoman vessel." [22]

England had achieved all her immediate aims. Lord Ponsonby had swept the Porte off its feet. It now expected its entire salvation from England. England would enforce the commercial treaty against the Pasha of Egypt. The English fleet would aid the Turkish squadron to destroy the Egyptian navy. England was only waiting for Reshid Pasha's arrival in London to conclude an offensive and defensive alliance with Turkey against the Viceroy. The Sultan seemed

[20] R. A., Nesselrode to Emperor, 23 October, 1838, o.s., *Rapports à l'Empereur,* folio 66, pp. 291-292.

[21] R. A., Rückmann to Divov, Constantinople, 16/28 August, 1838, folio 49, No. 106.

[22] R. A., Pahlen to Nesselrode, Paris, 30 September/12 October, 1838, folio 170, No. 83.

on the eve of the fulfillment of his most extravagant dreams of revenge. His exuberant imagination must have revelled in expectation of the long-awaited triumph over his hitherto successful rival.

But disenchantment was on its way. Scarcely had Reshid Pasha started for his goal than the rosy dream began to fade. Russia was still there, to the north, pressing upon the dilapidated fabric of the Ottoman Empire. On September 3, 1838, the long absent and sorely missed Russian minister to the Porte returned to Constantinople. Butenev was one of Nicolas's few diplomats of Russian origin. He was treated, perhaps on this account and perhaps because of his innate mildness, with a certain shade of condescension by his colleagues in the Russian service. He was by nature a person of compromise and indirection. He was at his best in inspiring confidence in Orientals, in learning the inner secrets of the Porte, in dealing with the Sultan through confidential servants. But he was not fitted to stand alone, to maintain Russia's isolated policy in Turkey even at the risk of war. In 1833 Count Orlov had been sent to Constantinople to put the required stiffness into the Russian negotiations. In 1839 there was no Orlov. Butenev, left to himself and unprovided with instructions for the unexpected events of July, 1839, took a decision which greatly limited Russia's future freedom of action in the Eastern Question. He signed the collective note to the Porte, of July 26, 1839. This step is not the crime against the Russian policy which has been depicted by Tatishchev and his followers. But it was a blunder, and Butenev committed it because of his inability to resist the pressure put upon him by unexpected circumstances and by the eagerness of his colleagues to undertake some collective action. In the autumn of 1838, however, Butenev was at his best. Then his job was to recover that intimate contact with the Sultan's favorite, which had been lost during his own absence. In a few months, he was able, if not to recover the preponderant position which Russia had claimed, but perhaps never possessed in reality, at least, to overthrow that new preponderance of English influence, which in September and October, 1838, seemed to cast its shadow across the Bosphorus.

At his first reception in the sultanic palace, Butenev found Mahmud much less expansive than usual. He spoke at length of the travels of the Russian reigning family, of his exquisite respect for the Emperor Nicolas. But he had nothing to say concerning the Egyptian question, nor about Reshid's mission to London. "I have in general been able to remark the same reserve in my explanations with the Turkish ministers. They are evidently dazzled by the prestige of the assurances and promises lavished on them of late by the English embassy and seem to expect from Reshid's mission results more important than they dare admit, for example, the disarming of the Pasha of Egypt and the recovery of Syria." Butenev was careful not to attack these dispositions front on, for that would only strengthen them, and betray Russia's own anxiety.[23] But a startling rumor soon forced Butenev to adopt a more aggressive policy. The report spread through Constantinople that the English fleet was to enter the

[23] R. A., Butenev to Nesselrode, Constantinople, 5/17 September, 1838, folio 50, No. 4.

Dardanelles. Some excuse, such as revictualling, could
be found, and it would be difficult for the Sultan, after
the ostentatious display of intimacy with the English,
to refuse. Butenev at once complained to the acting
minister for foreign affairs, Nouri Effendi, and to the
Sultan's latest favorite, Mustapha Bey, against the new
Turkish attitude of reserve towards him. The Sultan
hastened to reassure Butenev that he attached more
value than ever to close relations with Russia, and ap-
pointed Mustapha Bey to serve as a channel of direct
communication with himself, thus avoiding the more
formal channel of the ministry. Butenev at once made
use of this means to inquire about English projects
for entering the Dardanelles. The closing of the
Dardanelles to all foreign ships of war was the basis
of the treaty of Unkiar Iskelessi, and the condition
against which England had never ceased to protest.
The answer of the Sultan would determine whether that
treaty was still in force. "I therefore directed Prince
Handjéry to go immediately to Mustapha Bey, to
refer to these rumors, adding that I did not hesitate
to believe them baseless, but that I felt none the less
that it was my duty to warn His Highness against any
action or surprise which might be intended to introduce,
even for a moment, any English warships into the
Dardanelles: that such a fact, whatever pretext might
be adopted to lend it color, was of a nature to furnish
the most just motives of surprise and dissatisfaction
to the Imperial Court and to provoke, contrary to the
wish of His Highness, consequences so serious that it
might become the signal for that conflagration of the
Orient which the Porte and the Powers were so anxious

to prevent by all means in their power; that if, on the
one hand, the entrance of the English fleet into the
Dardanelles without any reasonable motive of utility
for the Porte, could not be regarded with indifference
by the Imperial Court, His Ally, on the other hand,
the mere news of an incident so fertile in incalculable
complications would be enough to satisfy all the wishes
of the Pasha of Egypt whose one desire was to find an
occasion suitable for accomplishing his projects of aggression and independence." Two days later the Sultan replied, assuring the Russian minister that "never,
under any pretext would he consent to allow an English
squadron to enter the Dardanelles; that no insinuation
to that effect had been made to date by the British
embassy and that, if it were made, it would be rejected
as it deserved; that if ever such an attempt were made
by surprise, the Porte could only see in it evidence of
hostility towards her and would hasten to come to an
agreement with the representative of the Imperial
Court as to the course it should pursue." The Sultan
again referred to the Toeplitz instructions as having
persuaded him that Russia would not object to the
junction of the Turkish and British fleets for the purpose of menacing the Pasha.[24]

This was a first and important result of the Russian
counter-offensive at Constantinople. The Sultan had
been reminded by his powerful ally that there were
some things that would not be tolerated, and the chief
of those was admitting the English fleet to the Dardanelles. The threats made by the Russian minister

[24] R. A., Butenev to Nesselrode, Constantinople, réservée, 21 Sep-
tember/2 October, folio 50, No. 11.

must have awakened him to a sense of his own danger; his worst nightmare must have been a fear of coordinated Russian and Egyptian aggrandizement. With Russia sweeping down upon the capital of the empire and Mohamed Ali conquering its Asiatic provinces, the Sultan might have been obliged to seek refuge on an English warship. Admitting the English fleet to the Straits, in violation of the 1833 treaty, would have been a direct provocation to Russia and Egypt to attack the Sultan. The Russian envoy needed, however, to see the joint cruise ended, and the English fleet well off to Malta, before he could sleep quietly of nights.

About the middle of October there was alarming news of preparations for an Anglo-Turk attack on Alexandria. The Turkish crews and soldiers were being vigorously drilled by English officers. Captain Tilden, an American in Turkish service, had declared that the combined naval forces would be adequate to capture Alexandria. But the Turkish ministers declared that the Grand Admiral had been ordered to refrain from any aggression or from offering any pretext for the Pasha to attack them.[25]

These alarming news and Palmerston's violent denunciations of Russian policy led Nicolas to give special attention to his diplomatic defenses at Constantinople. He was pleased with the declaration made by the Sultan through Mustapha Bey that he would never allow the English fleet to enter the Dardanelles, and, if such an attempt should be made by surprise, he would consult the Russian government as

[25] R. A., Butenev to Nesselrode, Constantinople, 6/18 October, 1838, folio 50, No. 15.

to its next course. This was satisfying, but Butenev must be firm because of the vacillating conduct of the Turkish ministers. He was to urge the Sultan to withdraw his fleet from its cruise with the English squadron. "Is it becoming to the interests and dignity of the Sultan to leave his fleet in the hands of the English and to render it, so to speak, hostage to the capricious and passionate policy of Lord Palmerston? . . . Another question which it would be beneficial to put to him will be: what would England say if the Emperor took it into his head to ask His Highness to put Russian officers on board the Turkish vessels, and how would the Sultan refuse to the Emperor, His Friend and Ally, a request which had just been granted to England?" The approach of winter offered a good excuse for withdrawing the Ottoman fleet to the Bosphorus without offending England. The Sultan should send away the English officers without any show or noise. ". . . As for the assurances which they [Butenev's despatches of 27 September/9 October] contain as to the Sultan's positive intention of keeping on his guard against any attempt the English might make to enter *under any pretext whatever* the channel of the Dardanelles, our August Master charges you formally to take note of it in His name and to declare to His Highness how much He is pleased to rely on the fidelity with which that Monarch will fulfill in this respect His obligations, which are, moreover, intimately connected with the interest of His own safety and of the dignity of Turkey." [26]

[26] R. A., Nesselrode to Butenev, to Constantinople, 27 October, 1838, o.s., folio 50, No. 1441.

In the meantime Butenev in Constantinople had been working to secure this very result. On October 23 he was able to inform his government that the Sultan had decided to recall his fleet to have it winter in the Bosphorus. The Porte was much disgruntled that the two combined fleets had cruised about the entrance to the Dardanelles, without even so much as demonstrating against the Pasha of Egypt. The British ambassador then urged Admiral Stopford to press farther to the south, as had been agreed on when the joint cruise had been undertaken. When Stopford replied that he had been ordered to bring his squadron back to Malta for the winter, the Sultan expressed his surprise and disappointment in a note to the Porte. "That junction of the two fleets has taken a singular turn. When it was decided on, at the time of Reshid Pasha's departure, it was intended to have the combined squadrons undertake a cruise as far as the waters of Alexandria and Syria. Now this cruise is limited to going and coming between Smyrna and the Dardanelles. One might think by this that the English fleet seems to wish to imitate the operations of the French fleet, which last year followed the trail of the Turkish fleet in all its movements. As all this has no purpose and no utility, let the order be given to the Capudan Pasha to bring back his fleet, to winter in Constantinople." [27]

Meanwhile the dispute over the Dardanelles had been transferred from Constantinople to London. Lord Palmerston referred to it in a stormy interview

[27] R. A., Butenev to Nesselrode, Constantinople, réservée, 11/23 October, 1838, folio 50, No. 18.

with Pozzo di Borgo. Palmerston "added that it had come to his knowledge that M. Butenev had declared that in case the English squadron should receive permission to come to Constantinople, that would be the signal for war. He claimed that the treaty forbade the entrance of the Straits only to the vessels of Powers at war with Russia, and that in peacetime the English squadron could even enter the Black Sea without our having the right to oppose it; I replied to him: so major and decisive a matter should not be examined in an abstract fashion, but appreciated according to the inevitable consequences which it would cause, and that I had too high an opinion of his prudence to imagine that he could authorize so extreme an act. By his vague reply he wished to persuade me that he had no such thing in mind." [28]

This menacing revival of old grievances in London reached Nesselrode on almost the same day with the news that the English admiral had actually left the bay of Smyrna for Malta and that the Capudan Pasha would return to Constantinople as soon as the last English ships left.[29] The Ottoman official gazette announced the return of the Turkish fleet without alluding to its junction with the English squadron. Such was the disappointment of the Sultan at the fruitlessness of the joint cruise.[30]

Ponsonby, too, was much disappointed at the recall

[28] R. A., Pozzo di Borgo to Nesselrode, London, 21 October/2 November, 1838, folio 130, No. 102.

[29] R. A., Butenev to Nesselrode, 20 October/1 November, 1838, folio 50, No. 23.

[30] R. A., Butenev to Nesselrode, Constantinople, 5/17 December, 1838, folio 50, No. 37.

of the British fleet. In October a private letter of his to Palmerston was opened by the very efficient secret service in Vienna. In it he wrote that the English squadron should not leave the Dardanelles and should be ready to act (i.e., against Russia) at the first signal. "That is the only means of inspiring respect in Russia; as soon as the fleet returns to Malta, Russia will again be able to lay down the law to the Ottoman Porte." [31] And the Russian ministry was not sorry to be able to pass on to the Porte a comment attributed to the English consul at Belgrade, who was trying to withdraw Prince Milosh of Serbia from Russian control. "He [Milosh] had nothing to apprehend from the Porte, since it would not dare to undertake anything against him at a moment when the Turkish fleet, joined to that of Great Britain, was in the hands of the English." [32]

The Russian government was not satisfied with the oral assurances given by the Sultan that the Porte would not allow any foreign warships to enter the Straits, and that if the Dardanelles were forced by surprise, it would consult first of all with the Russian government as to counter-measures. On November 29 a confidential notice was passed by the Russian ambassador to the Sultan's unofficial adviser. On December 11 he received a written reply restating the promise to keep the Straits closed.

The same communication settled another point in dispute. During the joint cruise of the two fleets

[31] R. A., Struve to Nesselrode, Vienna, chiffrée, 11/23 October, 1838, folio 217, No. 63.

[32] R. A., Nesselrode to Butenev, to Constantinople, 13 December, 1838, o.s., folio 50, No. 1483.

English officers had been placed on board the Turkish ships to instruct the officers and crews. Two of these officers had been engaged by the Turkish admiral as instructors. At the same time it was decided to send for a large number of naval instructors from England.[33] But when the Russian government protested against the presence of English officers in the Turkish service and dropped a hint that Russia might demand a similar privilege, the Porte took fright and hastily countermanded the order already despatched to London. If the English officers had started for the East, they were to be sent home, and in any case would not be admitted to Turkish service.[34] The Porte pretended that it had changed its own mind, but there was no doubt but that the reversal of decision had been wrought by Russian pressure.[35]

Shortly before, another conflict had arisen between Russia and England to perplex the Porte, over the protection given by Ponsonby to a Polish emigrant officer, Chrzanowski. In 1836 he had first visited Asia Minor, in English pay, to give an expert account of conditions prevailing there and, in particular, of Turkey's military state.[36] Under Russian pressure the Porte at last succeeded in having Chrzanowski leave the country. In May, 1838, he reappeared in Con-

[33] The initiative had been taken by the Porte in February, 1838; F. S. Rodkey, "Lord Palmerston and the Rejuvenation of Turkey, 1830-1841," in *Journal of Modern History*, I, iv, 588.

[34] Four officers reached Constantinople in March, 1839; only one received employment; Rodkey, *op. cit.*, pp. 589-590.

[35] R. A., Butenev to Nesselrode, Constantinople, 13/25 December, 1838, folio 50, No. 40.

[36] Hall, *op. cit.*, pp. 229-230; Rodkey, *op. cit.*, pp. 578, 584.

stantinople.   The animosity of the Russian cabinet towards this former Polish officer had in no wise diminished.   Ponsonby was alleged to have urged that he be attached to Hafiz Pasha, Turkish commander-in-chief in Anatolia, as military adviser.   Through the influence of Hozrew Pasha, the British embassy was brought to agree that he leave the country.[37]

An unofficial protest was made in London, and Lord Melbourne agreed that Palmerston and Ponsonby had acted very incautiously in sending back to Turkey a man against whom Russia had such serious grievances.   He promised that if he should be expelled again, England would not interfere to protect him.[38]

In August Ponsonby was still refusing to obey the timid wish expressed by the Porte to have Chrzanowski sent out of the country.[39]   But Russia had already protested to Turkey, and the Prussian minister for foreign affairs had likewise written from Toeplitz, where the sovereigns and cabinets of the three Powers were assembled, threatening to cut off the supply of Prussian instructors to the Turkish army if the Polish officer were not expelled.   Prussian officers could not serve together with a rebel against Russia, Prussia's ally.[40]

Finally, in October, when Russian influence began

[37] R. A., Rückmann to Nesselrode, secrète, 5/17 July, 1838, folio 48, No. 98.

[38] R. A., Pozzo di Borgo to Nesselrode, London, 11/23 August, 1838, folio 129, No. 80.

[37] R. A., Rückmann to Nesselrode, réservée, Constantinople, 20 August/1 September, 1838, folio 49, No. 109.

[40] R. A., Rückmann to Divov, réservée, Constantinople, 16/28 August, 1838, folio 49, No. 107.

to reassert itself against the temporary predominance established by Ponsonby over the Porte, the Sultan gave the positive order for Hafiz Pasha to send Chrzanowski away from his headquarters. Ponsonby was supposed to have directed him to leave via Bagdad to join the English forces in Persia. A pencil note was made on this despatch in Petersburg: "Immediately notify Count Simonich [Russian envoy in Teheran] of the arrival of this individual and demand his arrest by the Shah and his delivery to us for he is a *deserter*." [41]

But these quarrels over Polish officers and English instructors, and even over the possible admission of the English squadron to the Dardanelles, were only a part of the big question that was perplexing the Russian cabinet at that time. Was the Anglo-Turk treaty of August 16, 1838, purely a commercial treaty, or did it contain secret clauses destroying Russia's paramount position in the Ottoman Empire? Would Turkey fulfill the obligations of the 1833 treaty or had Russia lost the advantages gained at that time? As relations between Russia and England grew more and more tense during September and October, that was the question over which Russian diplomats were racking their brains with ever greater anxiety.

Immediately after receiving Pozzo di Borgo's alarming despatches of October, 1838, Nesselrode set about strengthening the Russian defenses in Constantinople. On November 8 he sent a very secret instruction to Butenev. The treaty of August 16 demanded thor-

---

[41] R. A., Butenev to Nesselrode, Constantinople, réservée, 27 September/9 October, 1838, folio 50, No. 12.

ough study and investigation. Its supposed purpose, the destruction of the economic resources of Mohamed Ali, had failed. "It remains for us to examine and to learn if the treaty . . . does not contain some clause still unknown to us and intended to neutralize the relations established between us and the Porte by virtue of our treaty of alliance. This is the doubt which the Emperor regards as doubly necessary to clear up at a moment when we see the English government actively engaged in causing difficulties for us everywhere and in sapping our influence abroad. Our August Master therefore expressly charges you with the duty of attentively sounding the ground in Constantinople, in order to find out whether the perfidious insinuations of the British ambassador have succeeded in shaking the political system thus far adopted by the Sultan and whether the transaction concluded by Lord Ponsonby binds him to any secret engagements, contrary to those contracted by the Porte towards us. . . . His Majesty wishes to know whether the confidence which He has placed thus far in the Sultan's intentions is still justified by the political conduct of this Sovereign, or whether a change in the attitude of the Porte may not compel us in turn to modify our own. This question, connected with our entire political system in the east, is too serious not to deserve to be the object of your most earnest meditations. Equally removed from premature anxiety as from blind security, we must seek to make clear the real situation of things at Constantinople, the progress which England may have made there in aims, hostile to us, finally, the consequences which such a change may cause in the political attitude of the Ottoman Porte. . . ." [42]

Butenev was able to reply that, to all evidence, there was no secret or political clause connected with the commercial treaty of August 16. Mr. Bulwer, the chief negotiator of the transaction, had spontaneously assured him that it contained no such clause. The French ambassador, before consenting to sign the treaty, in turn had made very careful investigations into this question.[43]

But there was another danger to Russian prestige at Constantinople. The Sultan was intent on securing a decision of the Powers of Europe in his favor. Palmerston was ardently courting the Porte and at the same time advocated the summoning of a European conference. Russia, the Sultan's ally, was the only convinced opponent of the conference idea. Might Ponsonby not make use of this inconsistency in the Russian position to strengthen his own position in Constantinople, at the expense of Russian prestige? In the beginning of October, 1838, Nesselrode instructed Butenev to warn the Porte against allowing itself to be drawn into a conference on the Eastern Question. The Russian minister drew up a memorandum for the personal information of the Sultan and transmitted it to him through Mustapha Bey. He reminded the Sultan that the conferences on Greece and Belgium had ended with the independence of the vassal and the

[42] R. A., Nesselrode to Butenev, to Constantinople, très secrète, 27 October, 1838, o.s., folio 50, No. 1442.

[43] R. A., Butenev to Nesselrode, Constantinople, très réservée, 22 November/4 December, 1838, folio 50, No. 31.

sacrifice of the legitimate rights of the sovereign. He indicated that this might be the result of a similar conference on the Egyptian question. He pointed out that the dignity and the interests of the Sultan would suffer if Mohamed Ali were invited to send a delegate on equal terms to this conference. These reasonings, however fallacious, had the desired effect. The order was at once sent to Reshid Pasha to refuse to enter a conference. When Reshid's assistant and partisan, Nouri Effendi, tried to postpone the despatch of these instructions by referring them to the dilatory Council of the Empire, Mustapha Bey himself took them to the Sultan for signature and they were sent off without delay. The conference idea was defeated as far as Turkish participation went.[44]

At the end of January, 1839, the conference danger assumed a new form. The Porte had begun secret and extensive preparations for an attack on Mohamed Ali in the spring. The representatives of the five Powers were unanimous in urging the Sultan to keep the peace and in warning him against the disastrous consequences to himself that would result from any act of aggression. The Porte itself was struck by the close unity of the five Powers.[45] This new development presented a certain pitfall to Russian policy. Nesselrode approved Butenev's cooperation thus far with the other representatives. At the same time, he warned him against a possible attempt to set up a conference at Constanti-

[44] R. A., Butenev to Nesselrode, Constantinople, réservée, 28 October/9 November, 1838, folio 50, No. 25.
[45] R. A., Butenev to Nesselrode, Constantinople, très réservée, 20 January/1 February, 1839, folio 45, No. 9.

nople, like that which Palmerston had tried in vain to establish in London the previous summer. "On the contrary, our cabinet must seek to preserve the advantage which it has always found in following an entirely independent course in respect to Turkish affairs." For the future Nesselrode laid down a different course of action. France and England might try to compel the Sultan to maintain the *status quo*. This would destroy their influence at the Porte. But Butenev was not to join in making such a threat, for Russia did not deny the Sultan's right to recover Syria. Russia would point out to the Sultan the dangers to himself arising from an act of aggression. Beyond that she would not go, but would leave to other Powers the onus of threatening the Sultan and of wounding his dignity as sovereign.[46] Here was an opportunity for Russia, less interested in Syria and Egypt than other Powers, to intrigue France and England into adopting a tone or measures which could only injure their own popularity with the Porte, for the ultimate benefit of Russia's influence.

It was not difficult for the Russian government to destroy Turkish illusions regarding a conference. It was a simple matter to point out that the combined cruise of the Turkish and English ships was useless to the Porte and even dangerous. The Sultan could promise to defend the Straits, for the English government itself did not intend to provoke a war by deliberately challenging Russia. But from August, 1838, there was one diplomatic enigma which the Russian

[46] R. A., Nesselrode to Butenev, to Constantinople, secrète, 14 February, 1839, o.s., folio 48, No. 1578.

diplomats could not solve. That was Reshid's mysterious mission to London. His sudden departure from Constantinople gave rise to extravagant rumors. Some said that the commercial treaty contained secret political clauses. Others said that a secret alliance had been formed and that Reshid expected to draw up its final provisions in London.[47] The Russians suspected, however, that his delay in reaching London showed that the direct political purpose of his journey inspired less hope in him and his master than it had in August, in the first intoxication of the rapprochement with England.

Reshid's progress from one capital to another was closely followed by Russian diplomacy. Metternich was the first to dash cold water on the Ottoman hopes for European support in an aggressive action against Mohamed Ali. He laughed outright at the naïve suggestion that the Viceroy could be persuaded to exchange his provinces for a sultanic pension and a palace on the beautiful Bosphorus. He could only advise the Porte to wait patiently for Mohamed Ali to die, and then to claim his provinces for the Sultan. Reshid's despatch to the Porte, announcing the poor success with which he had met in Vienna, was intercepted and deciphered by the Austrian secret bureau.[48] At Berlin Reshid was advised by Baron Werther, the foreign minister, to let Egyptian affairs rest; he urged on the Turkish minister the great benefits derived by Turkey

[47] It is significant that the first formal proposal of an Anglo-Turk entente was advanced by Turkey as early as April, 1837; Rodkey, *op. cit.*, p. 586.

[48] R. A., Struve to Nesselrode, Vienna, 18/30 October, 1838, folio 217, No. 66.

from her alliance with Russia. Reshid replied that the Porte wished to have friends everywhere.[49] Reshid's arrival had been preceded by rumors that an offensive and defensive alliance had been signed between England and Turkey. But Reshid hastened to deny to the Russian minister that the commercial treaty of August 16, 1838, contained any secret or political articles.[50]

The Russian panic over Reshid's mysterious mission now began to be allayed. The Turkish ministers themselves pointed out to Butenev the unusual wording of the Sultanic rescript, directing him to embark on his diplomatic pilgrimage. It read that, if Reshid failed in his efforts, the failure should fall on him alone. This was a plain hint that the Porte did not put much faith in the exaggerated hopes inspired by the Turkish-English rapprochement. Within a few weeks of his departure, Reshid was openly ridiculed by Mustapha Bey, the newest favorite of the Sultan, and his most powerful rivals in the ministry were predicting his failure.[51] At the same time, the Porte had come to realize that English motives in pressing for a rapprochement were not entirely altruistic. Mustapha Bey confided his new suspicions to the Russian minister. "It is now plain that Lord Ponsonby has been so violent and uncontrolled against Russia of late only because of England's complications with Persia, which he attributed to the incitement of Russian agents. Now

[49] R. A., Ribeaupierre to Nesselrode, Berlin, 16/28 October, 1838, folio 38, No. 110.

[50] R. A., Ribeaupierre to Nesselrode, Berlin, 9/21 October, 1838, and 18/30 October, 1838, folio 38, No. 103 and No. 111.

[51] R. A., Butenev to Nesselrode, Constantinople, très réservée, 11/23 October, 1838, folio 50, No. 17.

that these Persian affairs seemed to be arranged to suit him, that ambassador has at once quieted down, which is one more proof that at bottom he cares very little about Turkey's interests." [52]

Ponsonby's enthusiasm for the Turkish alliance may never have been very deep. In January, 1839, he was as insistent as the other four ministers at Constantinople that the Sultan keep the peace. He admitted to the Austrian Internuncio that he was absolutely ignorant of Reshid's negotiations in London and did not look upon them with any great hope.[53] Ponsonby may even have regarded the negotiations in London as a means of gaining time and of delaying any extreme decisions by the Sultan. On January 27, during the week when Mahmud seemed determined on war, he urged the Porte to take no decisive steps before receiving the results of Reshid's mission.[54] By the end of February, 1839, Reshid Pasha was able to report progress to his impatient sovereign. His despatches were received with the greatest interest and led to unusual activity at the Porte. At first the Russian minister was unable to secure any information. Mustapha Bey, his previous channel of communication, was now in semi-disgrace, probably because of his too great sincerity in urging the need for peace.[55] A week later Butenev had much

[52] R. A., Butenev to Nesselrode, Constantinople, réservée, 28 October/9 November, 1838, folio 50, No. 25.

[53] R. A., Butenev to Nesselrode, Constantinople, particulière, 20 January/1 February, 1839, folio 45, pp. 642-644; Stürmer's summary of conversation with Ponsonby.

[54] *British Parliamentary Papers,* Correspondence Relative to the Affairs of the Levant, Series I, London, 1841, XXIX, 2.

[55] R. A., Butenev to Nesselrode, Constantinople, réservée, 23 February/7 March, 1839, folio 45, No. 27.

more satisfactory information to report to his government.

An unmentioned, but reliable, source had informed him of the contents of Reshid's reports. Palmerston was very favorable to the idea of aiding the Sultan against Mohamed Ali. On the other hand, England was bound by the diplomatic steps of the preceding summer to follow the line of conduct of the other Powers. Her situation in Europe would be compromised if she claimed the right of sole interference in Egypt. But Palmerston asked Reshid to write to the Sultan that if he really desired England's effective cooperation against Mohamed Ali, he should authorize his ambassador in London to conclude a formal treaty of alliance. In that case, England would be ready, not only to repeat the imposing naval demonstration of the preceding year, but also to force Mohamed Ali to reduce his naval armaments to a degree which would no longer be dangerous for the Sultan's government. Although the Sultan was greedy of any means which might serve to destroy Mohamed Ali, he was but poorly satisfied with Palmerston's proposal. He therefore authorized Reshid Pasha to enter into negotiations, but with the greatest circumspection, and without hastening to accept any final engagements.

Just as Butenev had succeeded in persuading Reshid's enemies at the Porte, in October, 1838, to limit his freedom of action by forbidding him to enter a conference, he was now successful in circumscribing that minister's freedom of action in the negotiations which were about to be renewed. On March 8 these additional and confidential instructions were despatched

to London. They pointed out to Reshid that England
had been trying systematically to injure Turkey's relations with Russia. He was not to allow Palmerston
to insert into the treaty any clauses contrary to Turkey's engagements to Russia. For example, there could
be no question of admitting English ships to the Dardanelles, in violation of the Russian alliance. Reshid was
instructed, in addition, to sign nothing before securing
the approval of the Porte.[56] The negotiation between
England and Turkey would go on. Russia could not
prevent that, for the Sultan was eager to grasp any
hand stretched out to him in his predicament. But
Butenev believed that Reshid Pasha would now not
dare to accept any commitments dangerous to Russia.

Only four days later Ponsonby wrote to his government that another report had been received from Reshid.
He now informed his government that nothing was to
be expected from the courts of London and Paris.[57]
Meanwhile, the Russian government had found a new
means for attacking Reshid's position. His colleague
and partisan in Paris, Feth-Akhmet Pasha, had been
speaking in a very slighting way of the Russo-Turkish
alliance. He had declared that England was already
disposed to enter a plan for breaking off that alliance
and was urging France to join it. Nesselrode asked
Butenev to point out that, if the Turkish representatives abroad wished to maintain the prestige of their
government, they must not criticize an alliance, the
personal achievement of the Sultan; and, if they wished

56 R. A., Butenev to Nesselrode, Constantinople, très réservée,
3/15 March, 1839, folio 45, No. 29.

57 *Parl. Papers,* 1841, XXIX, 8.

to preserve the tranquillity of the empire, they should not invite foreign interference into matters which concerned the Sultan alone.[58]   In the first week of April Butenev was able to report that the Sultan had been justly incensed by the expressions of his representative in Paris; in addition, a copy of the reprimand to Feth-Ahkmet Pasha was to be sent to Reshid in London, as a warning.[59]

In the first week of April fresh despatches were received from London.   Reshid was now able to state more clearly the conditions offered by Palmerston.   In case Mohamed Ali declared his independence, England would lend her assistance to the Sultan.   The two fleets would act in common against the coasts of Syria and Egypt; the Porte would declare a blockade in its own name; any Egyptian ships, whether ships of war or merchant vessels, would be turned over to the Sultan by the English squadron.   The first interpreter of the Russian embassy was allowed to read Reshid's confidential explanations.   He wrote that it was impossible for any one Power aggressively to come to the aid of the Sultan without leaguing the other Powers against itself.   At the same time, Russia and France were both making advances to England, despite the French inclination manifested just previously for a rapprochement with Russia.   England was convinced that France could not consent to use force against the Pasha of Egypt; the Porte, therefore, should not alarm France

[58] R. A., Nesselrode to Butenev, to Constantinople, confidentielle, 14 February, 1839, o.s., folio 48, No. 1579.
[59] R. A., Butenev to Nesselrode, Constantinople, 21 March/2 April, 1839, folio 45, No. 40.

by demanding too much of her. If England should wish to act alone against Egypt, Russia and France would probably join forces against her. It was, therefore, essential to unite both France and England to the Porte by a defensive alliance; later, these Powers might consent to act more vigorously in defense of the Sultan's interests. The only thing for the Porte to do, then, was to conclude the defensive alliance now, and then wait for circumstances to arise, under which France and England could be persuaded to aid her actively.

Reshid's information was accurate, but it did not satisfy the Sultan. Although Butenev knew that the Turkish sovereign was greatly disappointed, he decided not to leave the decision of the council to chance. He sent his first interpreter to Riza Bey, the new and only confidant of the Sultan, and warned him of the dangers which menaced the Sultan. If this mysterious negotiation for an alliance in London were continued, it would certainly cause the greatest displeasure in Petersburg and might react in a most unfavorable way on the situation of the Porte. Riza Bey assured the Russian agent that the Sultan held steadfastly to his alliance with Russia.[60]

Whatever impression the Russian message may have made, it was certain that the Sultan was not to be satisfied with the innocuous conditions proposed by Palmerston. The Sultan was determined to recover the provinces held by Mohamed Ali and nothing short of an offensive alliance would have suited him. And he

[60] R. A., Butenev to Nesselrode, Constantinople, très réservée, 25 March/6 April, 1839, folio 45, No. 45.

must have guessed that for Palmerston, at least, the negotiation of an alliance with England was regarded as the best means for delaying the outbreak of hostilities between the Porte and its vassal. On April 6, 1839, Ponsonby had to report to his government that "the Sublime Porte could not be satisfied with the treaty, because it is not the treaty which Reshid Pasha wished to make; that the Porte desired to destroy the *status quo*, and the treaty proposed by Lord Palmerston not only leaves it in full force, but also binds the Porte not to take advantage in future of any favorable occasion that may offer . . ." [61] On perceiving that its negotiations with England would not lead to the result desired, the Porte took two important decisions. In the first place, it ordered Hafiz Pasha to advance into Syrian territory, thus making unavoidable the outbreak of hostilities and the battle of Nézib. At the same time the Sultan resolved to lay bare Reshid's entire negotiation to his Russian ally, in order to destroy the bad impression created by his flirtation with England, and to win Russian support for his attack on Mohamed Ali. The Russians now attributed to themselves especial merit in breaking up Reshid's negotiation. Actually, the comparison of dates shows that it was not until the Porte was obliged to abandon hope of securing aggressive support from England, that the Sultan resolved to lay down his cards to Russia.

During April Ponsonby wrestled with the ministers of the Porte, to convince them that the Sultan should accept the defensive alliance proposed by Palmerston

[61] *Parl. Papers,* 1841, XXIX, 11.

and should not begin hostilities.[62]   By April 22 it was
plain that the Sultan had refused Reshid's treaty
draft.   Even the sketch of the treaty, retranslated
from the Turkish for Ponsonby, showed in what an
elementary stage the negotiations still lingered.   The
rough draft contained only three clauses, and merely
provided for common action by the Turkish and English fleets.[63]   At the same time, the Porte was loath to
confess its failure to the foreign representatives.
Nouri Effendi told the Austrian Internuncio that there
were still hopes for Reshid's success in London.[64]
From April 10 to 16 the Porte and the Sultan debated
what their course should be.   Finally, it was decided
that the terms of the proposed treaty were entirely
inadequate for the needs of the Empire.   Thereupon,
the draft of the treaty was communicated to the Russian minister.   It is the same as that published in the
English Parliamentary Papers, and leaves no doubt,
but that it represented the final draft drawn up by
Palmerston and Reshid.   By April 16, new instructions were sent to Reshid, and at the same time communicated officially to the Russian representative.
Reshid was to break off the negotiation with the English
ministry.   The excuse was to be created by raising the
demands of the Sultan.   He now insisted that the
restoration of Syria to his own direct rule must be introduced into the proposed alliance.   The Sultan ex-

[62] At the same time Ponsonby was arguing eloquently in his
despatches to Palmerston, in defense of the Sultan's cause; Rodkey,
op. cit., p. 591.

[63] *Parl. Papers,* 1841, XXIX, 12-14.

[64] *Parl. Papers,* 1841, XXIX, 15.

pected that this would automatically bring the negotiations to an end, and directed Reshid to return at
once to Constantinople. It was added confidentially,
however, that, if the sudden departure of Reshid
threatened to turn Palmerston against the Porte, his
withdrawal might be prepared gradually. The Sultan
had now abandoned all hope of drawing England into
an offensive alliance. At the same time he remained
true to his "see-saw" policy by representing his own
diplomatic defeat as a concession to Russia.[65]

Reshid's information about the relations of the different Powers and about England's reluctance to take
the initiative of aggressive measures had not deterred
the Sultan from acting to satisfy his constant desire
for vengeance. It had a contrary effect. At the moment when the first hostile steps were taken, the Sultan
appealed to all the Powers to aid him in reducing "that
perverse man," Mohamed Ali, to the position, "from
which he ought never to have been allowed to rise." [66]
Palmerston's positive refusal to assist the Sultan if he
began the war against the Pasha, was now received in
the middle of May, and annihilated whatever hopes the
Sultan still entertained of securing the isolated assistance of England.[67]

The Russian vice-chancellor was greatly pleased with
the results achieved by Butenev at Constantinople. In
a despatch of April 10, 1839, Nesselrode expressed his
satisfaction that the Sultan had ordered that the pro-

[65] R. A., Butenev to Nesselrode, Constantinople, 13/25 April, 1839,
très secrète, folio 46, No. 56.

[66] *Parl. Papers,* 1841, XXIX, 21-23; R. A., Butenev to Nesselrode,
Constantinople, très réservée, 9/21 May, 1839, folio 46, No. 68.

[67] *Parl. Papers,* 1841, XXIX, 4, 28.

posed alliance with England should not contain any
clauses contrary to the alliance with Russia, especially
in regard to the Dardanelles.   At the same time,
Russia ordered her agent in Egypt to warn and threaten
the Pasha against disturbing the peace.   One object of
this new step was to show the Sultan that England was
no more zealous than Russia itself in defending the
security of Turkey.   At the same time, as regarded the
Sultan's plans of aggression, Russia could only warn
him of the dangers inseparable from such projects,
without using threats.[68]   Nor was the Russian cabinet
content merely to approve its minister's steps at the
Porte.   Nesselrode had already written a confidential
letter to his representative in London.   Pozzo di Borgo
was warned to watch Reshid's negotiations as closely
as possible, and to try to defeat them.   It was also
important not to compromise Russia's secret source of
information at Constantinople.[69]   By the first week
in May the Russian government was ready to act
more vigorously in London.   Count Orlov, the Russian commander on the Bosphorus in 1833, and well
known to the Turks, was to visit London with the
Grand Duke Alexander.   By a despatch of May 4,
1839, Orlov was directed to take advantage of his stay
in England to have a decisive interview with Reshid
Pasha.   The Ottoman representative had not abandoned the idea of drawing up a definitive alliance between the Porte and England.   On April 26, before

[68] R. A., Nesselrode to Butenev, réservée, to Constantinople, 29
March, 1839, o.s., folio 48, No. 1654.
[69] R. A., Nesselrode to Pozzo di Borgo, to London, particulière,
24 March, 1839, o.s., folio 121, pp. 519-520.

he could have received the Porte's new instructions of
April 16, he wrote a note to Palmerston, pressing him
to communicate the final draft of the alliance, as the
English minister had promised some time before. Palmerston replied only on May 6, and then he could only
promise to have the draft ready in a few days.[70] Palmerston was hindered from fulfilling his promise by
the parliamentary crisis which occurred in May, 1839,
and by the visit of the Russian Grand Duke. In any
case, Pozzo di Borgo and Orlov received Nesselrode's
instructions of May 4, on the 17. "Count Orlov's
presence in London has seemed to us a very opportune
circumstance to convey a salutary reprimand to the
Ottoman ambassador, to influence him strongly by fear
of seeing his schemes represented in the Sultan's eyes
as a combination diametrically opposed to the system
of alliance adopted by that sovereign himself towards
Russia. The personal credit enjoyed by Count Orlov
at Constantinople and the services rendered by him to
the Sultan enable him to speak to Reshid Pasha in the
most peremptory language, by letting him suspect
the possibility of a direct appeal made by Count Orlov
to the Sultan to denounce the perfidious conduct of his
ambassador." Let Reshid see that you are informed
of the reprimand administered by the Sultan to Feth-
Akhmet Pasha, in Paris, "in order that Reshid Pasha
may know that our cabinet has its attention seriously
fixed on the actions of the Ottoman representatives and
that it possesses at Constantinople all the means neces-

[70] *Parl. Papers,* 1841, XXIX, 9-10.

sary to make them return to the line of their duties, as soon as they try to depart from it." [71]

On receiving the first warning of Reshid's intrigues, Pozzo di Borgo had had a very unsatisfactory interview with him. Reshid agreed with Pozzo that the Turkish empire needed repose above all else. Pozzo doubted that Reshid was sincere in saying this, since as a reformer of the empire and the partisan of the English alliance, he must belong to the group of agitators. Pozzo di Borgo, here again, was ready to picture the worst as lying ahead. "The slightest reflection should suffice to prove to the Sultan the dangers of the English alliance, for Russia would take the initiative against him and put in security the points which she would never allow to be occupied by the arms of other Powers, either provisionally . . . or definitively." But the Sultan would not dare to enter into an alliance against Russia. "The arm which can save us from the defection of the Porte and from the advantage which England would chiefly like to derive from that, is entirely in our own forces. If Mahmud foresees his own ruin in his treason, he will refrain from it. That is the only motive which can restrain his hatred for the Pasha and, at bottom, against us; for, despite the fact that His Majesty the Emperor has saved the Sultan and the Turkish empire from downfall and final dissolution by stopping Ibrahim Pasha, gratitude will not wipe out ancient hatreds nor the humiliation caused by the precautions which the Turks are obliged to take every

[71] R. A., Nesselrode to Pozzo di Borgo, to London, très secrète, 22 April, 1839, o.s., folio 121, No. 1693.

day." [72]   At the beginning of May, Reshid Pasha had
already received his new instructions from Constantinople.   He now told Pozzo di Borgo that he "had
nothing more to do in London."   He defended himself
against the accusation of being anti-Russian.   The
Russian representative took alarm at the new influence
that Reshid seemed likely to acquire on returning to
Constantinople to take up again his functions as minister of foreign affairs.[73]

When the Russian instructions of May 4 reached
London, the cabinet crisis was over.   Much to Pozzo
di Borgo's disappointment he still had to treat business
with Palmerston.   The Queen's stubbornness in refusing to allow Sir Robert Peel to change her ladies-in-
waiting had given the only half willing Conservative
leaders the chance to withdraw and had allowed the all
too willing Liberals to recover office.   At the same
time Count Orlov took occasion to speak very severely
to Reshid and thus to destroy any further desire which
he might have to negotiate a treaty with England or
France.   Reshid replied that he would be leaving soon
for Constantinople, and that he had waited in London
only to see how the ministerial crisis ended.   Pozzo di
Borgo was much alarmed by Reshid's admission that
the treaty proposed by Palmerston was to be only an
opening.   That meant that Reshid still hoped to draw
England and France to assist the Sultan actively
against the Pasha of Egypt.   But the real danger,

[72] R. A., Pozzo di Borgo to Nesselrode, London, 11/23 April, 1839,
folio 119, No. 41.

[73] R. A., Pozzo di Borgo to Nesselrode, London, 28 April/10 May,
1839, folio 120, No. 48.

the Russian ambassador believed, lay in the certainty
that these two Powers would not be brought to make
such sacrifices for the Sultan, unless the latter con-
sented to join them in opposition to Russia and in
violation of the Russo-Turkish alliance.   The return
of Reshid to Constantinople therefore left him filled
with foreboding of evil for the Russian position in
Turkey.[74]

The long months of Anglo-Turkish negotiation had
therefore come back to the starting-point.   The English had seemed, in August, 1838, willing to aid the
Sultan actively in subjecting his too powerful vassal.
When the scare of war with Russia had quieted down,
the English government lost interest in its flirtation
with the Porte.   Between August, 1838, when Reshid
started on his mission, and February, 1839, when
negotiations actually opened in London, the position
of the English government had changed considerably.
In August the rapprochement with Turkey seemed an
essential means for threatening both Persia and Russia.
By the winter of 1839, the English interest in any
immediate steps in Persia had disappeared.   In the
summer of 1838 it had seemed necessary to be able to
menace Persia with the danger of a civil war, begun on
Turkish soil by Zel-u-Sultan.   In February, 1839,
Palmerston was satisfied to let the settlement of the
Persian affairs rest until the campaign in Afghanistan
was over.   And the Russian abandonment of the too
exposed positions taken by her agents in Persia and
Afghanistan satisfied the London cabinet that there was

[74] R. A., Pozzo di Borgo to Nesselrode, London, particulière, 5/17
May, 1839, and 19/31 May, 1839, No. 59, in folio 120.

no need to threaten Russia with the conclusion of an Anglo-Turk alliance, which would, by its nature, be directed as much against Russia as against Egypt. On the other hand, from January, 1839, Palmerston wished to utilize the negotiation in London as a means for delaying the outbreak of hostilities in the Levant. The draft of the alliance, so elementary and incomplete in its terms, was obviously intended to persuade the Sultan to continue negotiations, while letting slip by the opportunity for military operations in 1839. For England, with her forces engaged in China, Afghanistan, Aden, Karak, and Canada, the possibility of new complications in the Levant was not a pleasing one. That the failure to secure an offensive alliance with England only spurred the Sultan to try his fate by arms, was no fault of Palmerston's.

For Russia the results of this year of negotiation and intrigue were less consoling. The continuous series of steps taken by the Porte to woo English support proved that the foundation of the Russo-Turkish alliance was not firm. It proved that Turkey was bound to Russia chiefly by fear, and also by the impossibility, for the time being, of replacing the Russian alliance with any other. Such an uncertain equilibrium of influence at the Porte could not last. Russia had received a warning that her alliance with Turkey would not give her that permanent and exclusive influence over Ottoman policy, for which she had hoped in 1833. The willingness of the Russian government, in August, 1839, to give up her burdensome and, at bottom, merely nominal, preponderance at Constantinople, can be traced to the experience of the preceding winter.

For Turkey this winter had brought different lessons. It had shown her that European policy was so closely bound together that she could not hope that any one Power, however friendly to her, would intervene aggressively in her favor. The jealousy of the other Powers would force that one Power, be it England or Russia, to give up the attempt to protect and enlarge the dominions of the Sultan at the expense of Mohamed Ali. The eagerness of the Porte to throw itself on the cooperative advice and support of all the Powers, in July, 1839, can be traced to this lesson, as much as to the complete defencelessness of the twice defeated government. For the moment, however, Sultan Mahmud was unwilling to recognize his real plight. The refusal of England to assist him in his plans of aggression only made him the more determined to risk everything on his own forces. The refusal of the English, the warnings of the Russians and Austrians, the recognized partiality of France for Mohamed Ali did not deter him from the dangerous and fatalistic course which he had chosen.

VII

Reopening of the Eastern Crisis in 1839

By the end of April, 1839, the eastern crisis had entered upon a new and active phase, with the crossing of the Turkish army under Hafiz Pasha into Syrian territory. The outcome of the struggle between the armies of the Sultan and Mohamed Ali would decide the future, not only of the Near East, but also of the European equilibrium of power. Would the Pasha make good his threat to push on to Constantinople? Would a new Russian descent on the Bosphorus be contested only by diplomatic means by England and France? Would Austria be obliged to take sides in a European struggle over the partition of Turkey, or would Metternich manœuvre all the Powers into a conference? All these possibilities were latent in the situation both in 1838 and in 1839. In 1838 Austria showed more openly than before a tendency to support England and France in the east. The difference in viewpoint between the cabinets of London and Paris was evident as early as June, 1838. The refusal of Russia to be drawn into a European conference had inflamed English suspicions. On the other hand, with the support of the three Eastern Powers, Palmerston had been able to settle the Belgian question without real cooperation by the French government and in despite of a large and noisy section of French opinion. The question of Persia and Afghanistan had bulked large during the whole of 1838, but the danger-point in Anglo-Russian relations had been passed by the opening of 1839. The struggle for paramount influence over Turkish policy had convinced both England and Russia that permanent geographical and political factors made it impossible for either one to exclude the other completely from influence over the government of the Sultan. In 1838 Palmerston had foreseen only two alternatives: subjection of Russian policy to a European conference, or war with Russia. Russia had defeated his attempt to establish a conference on the Eastern Question, and had shown reluctance to be drawn into a European war. The apparently fruitless wrangling of 1838 had, however, brought to light certain parallel tendencies in both Russian and English policy. Their struggle had cleared the ground for cooperation in 1839 and 1840 in a definite and restricted program for strengthening Turkey against Mohamed Ali, and thus of postponing for nearly a generation the struggle which in 1838 appeared imminent to both.

APPENDICES

Appendix A

[R. A., Menshikov to Nesselrode, *Reports to Emperor*, 4 January, 1838, o.s., folio 66, pp. 2-16.]

L'Empereur m'a chargé de Vous prévenir, Monsieur le Comte, que S. M. a l'intention d'expédier au printems pro- chain deux vaisseaux de ligne avec un ou deux avisos qui partiraient de la Baltique sous prétexte d'évolutions et se rendraient ensuite aux Dardanelles pour passer dans la Mer Noire.

La longueur de cette navigation exige une relâche pour rafraîchir les équipages et faire des vivres et de l'eau. Dans les circonstances présentes les ports des Îles de Sar- daigne me semble être les seuls à désigner pour cette relâche. J'attendrai Vos communications sur les décisions ultérieures de l'Empereur pour faire le projet d'instruc- tions à donner à l'officier qui commandera cette escadre.

[Nesselrode's report to the Emperor, 16 January, 1838, o. s.]

Le Prince Menchikoff m'a prévenu, qu'il est de l'inten- tion de Votre Majesté d'expédier au printems prochain deux vaisseaux de ligne avec un ou deux avisos qui par- tiraient de la Baltique, relâcheraient dans l'un des ports de la Sardaigne et se rendraient de là aux Dardanelles pour passer dans la Mer Noire.

En me fesant connaître éventuellement ces dispositions par le billet ci-joint, M. le Ministre de la Marine a bien voulu m'annoncer, qu'il attendrait de ma part une com- munication sur les décisions ultérieures de Votre Majesté, afin d'y conformer les instructions dont il aurait à munir le commandant de cette escadre.

Je me fais un devoir, Sire, de solliciter en conséquence Vos ordres sur cet objet, en tant qu'il réclame le concours du Ministère des Affaires Étrangères.

J'oserai à cette occasion observer avant tout, que les relations amicales heureusement établies entre le Cabinet Impérial et celui de Turin, nous autorisent à compter d'avance sur l'empressemen avec lequel le Roi de Sardaigne accueillera les démarches que Notre Ministre sera chargé de faire pour annoncer l'arrivée de notre escadre et pour obtenir durant sa relâche dans les ports Sardes toutes les facilités désirables. Dans cette attente, je ne saurais douter du résultat complètement satisfesant des ouvertures, dont M. d'Obrescoff aurait à s'acquitter dèsque Votre Majesté daignera me charger de lui en transmettre l'ordre.

Quant au passage de notre escadre par le Bosphore, le sentiment de mon devoir et le dévouement profond qui m'anime pour Votre service, Sire, me commandent de Vous exposer à cet égard quelques considérations qui se rattachent au système général de Votre politique ; considérations très graves que ma propre responsabilité, comme serviteur fidèle de Votre Majesté, m'oblige à soumettre préalablement à Ses décisions avec une respectueuse et entière franchise.

Au milieu des circonstances difficiles et souvent dangereuses où se sont trouvées les affaires de l'Orient, Votre Majesté a invariablement adopté pour principe de mettre à couvert la sûreté des provinces méridionales de la Russie, en veillant rigoureusement à ce que l'entrée des Dardanelles restât fermée au pavillon de guerre étranger.

Ce principe, d'accord avec les intérêts bien entendus et avec les anciennes traditions politiques de la Porte, a été consacré formellement par le traité conclu entre la Turquie et l'Angleterre en 1809.

Par cette transaction, le principe de la fermeture des Dardanelles est clairement reconnu "comme une ancienne règle de l'Empire Ottoman qui doit être observé en tems de paix vis-à-vis de toute puissance, quelle que ce soit, principe auquel la Cour Britannique promet aussi de se conformer."

Cependant il n'existait pas jusqu'alors un *engagement direct* par lequel la Porte fût tenue *envers nous* de maintenir également la fermeture des Dardanelles *en cas de guerre* entre la Russie et d'autres Puissances.

C'est cette lacune que notre traité d'alliance du 26 Juin/8 Juillet 1833 a servi à combler.

L'article secret de ce traité stipule que la Turquie "à la place du secours qu'elle doit prêter à la Russie en vertu du traité patent, bornera son action en faveur de la cour Impériale à fermer le détroit des Dardanelles, c.à.d., à ne permettre à aucun bâtiment de guerre étranger d'y entrer sous aucun prétexte quelconque."

Vainement les Puissances maritimes ont-elles cherché à invalider notre traité d'alliance. Nos efforts ont réussi à inspirer au Sultan la fermeté et le courage de maintenir ses engagements envers nous dans toute leur intégrité.

Mais afin de mettre la Porte en mesure de persister dans cette attitude, Votre Majesté a toujours eu loyalement en vue de ne stipuler et de ne point exiger en notre faveur ce même droit de passage des Dardanelles que nous avions un si grand intérêt à voir refuser à toutes les autres Puissances.

Il en est résulté que dans l'état actuel de nos relations avec la Turquie, les traités obligent celle-ci *à fermer* au pavillon de guerre étranger l'entrée des Dardanelles, mais ces transactions ne l'obligent nullement à nous *l'ouvrir* à nous mêmes.

Le traité d'Andrinople, confirmé par celui de Constantinople, ne stipule explicitement en notre faveur, que le libre passage de bâtiments *marchands;* mais aucune stipulation ne nous autorise à exiger, dans le Bosphore, l'admission de nos *bâtiments de guerre*.

Tel est le principe général qui sert de base à nos transactions sur cette importante matière.

Ce n'est que par une exception spéciale et par pure déférence pour nous que le Gouvt. Ottoman nous accorde de tems en tems la faculté de relever notre station en Grèce et nous délivre à cet effet des firmans de passage pour les bâtiments légers qui reviennent de l'Archipel, ainsi que pour ceux qui vont les remplacer en venant de la mer Noire.

Jusqu'ici la Porte ne nous a jamais refusé cette facilité comme elle en aurait rigoureusement le droit, selon la lettre de nos traités.

De notre côté nous n'avons jamais usé de cette facilité qu'avec ménagement, à de longs intervalles, sans éclat. De cette manière le trajet de nos bâtiments venant de l'Archipel pour se rendre dans la mer Noire a passé jusqu'ici et continue à passer comme un fait inaperçu, comme une mesure exceptionnelle, justifiée par le besoin de renouveler périodiquement la station des bâtiments légers qui sont destinés à entretenir le service de notre correspondance habituelle avec la Grèce.

Mais il en serait tout autrement d'une escadre, partie de la Baltique, qui, après avoir fait le tour de l'Europe et attiré les regards de toutes les Puissances maritimes viendrait se présenter devant les Dardanelles et demanderait à traverser le canal de Constantinople.

Il arriverait alors nécessairement de deux choses l'une: ou bien la Porte nous refuserait le passage; ou bien elle se déciderait à nous l'accorder.

Dans le premier cas, nous n'aurions, ainsi que je l'ai déjà observé, aucun droit positif pour *insister* sur le passage. La Porte en déclinant notre demande se renfermerait dans l'exécution stricte des traités. Elle serait légalement dans son droit. Nous n'aurions rien à objecter contre son refus. Mais quels que soient les ménagements dont elle ne manquerait pas de l'accompagner, il n'en est pas moins vrai qu'aux yeux de l'Europe, un pareil refus aurait quelque chose de blessant pour la dignité de la Russie. Il en résulterait pour nous le double désavantage: d'une part d'avoir porté une atteinte sensible à notre crédit; de l'autre, d'avoir fait naître un grief et provoqué un motif de mésintelligence qui ne pourrait manquer de réagir d'une manière fâcheuse sur nos relations directes avec la Turquie.

Dans le second cas, en admettant que le Sultan nous accorde le passage. L'Angleterre et la France saisiraient avec empressement ce prétexte pour demander à leur tour à la Porte la permission de faire entrer quelques bâtiments de guerre dans la mer Noire. L'Angleterre profiterait d'autant plus de cette circonstance qu'elle prétendrait avoir besoin d'accorder à son commerce dans ces parages la protection d'une station navale; combinaison qui déjà a été soulevée une fois au sein du Parlement et que le Ministère se féliciterait sans doute de réaliser, au gré de l'opinion publique, dès l'instant où nous lui en fournirions l'occasion. Le Gouvernement Ottoman, nous devons nous y attendre, n'aurait alors ni la force ni le courage de résister à cette demande des Puissances maritimes. Notre mission s'efforcerait vainement d'objecter, que la Mer Noire n'est environnée de toute part que de provinces soumises à la domination des deux Puissances, la Russie et la Porte; que nos bâtiments de guerre rentrent dans *nos* ports, sans que leur présence puisse y menacer une Puissance tierce quelconque, tandisque l'apparition du pavillon de guerre Anglais ou Français dans ces mêmes parages ne pourrait être dirigée ouvertement que contre nous. Tous ces argumens que notre mission ne manquerait certainement pas de faire valoir avec le langage de la vérité et de la raison, tomberaient néanmoins devant une objection invincible: c'est que la Porte n'a pas le pouvoir de refuser à l'Angleterre et à la France une concession que nous aurions exigée nous-mêmes en dehors de la lettre des traités. Ainsi pour justifier sa faiblesse, pour excuser sa pusillanimité, la Porte nous dirait que notre Cabinet ne saurait le blâmer si, en ouvrant l'entrée des Dardanelles à l'Angleterre et à la France, elle se résigne à dévier malgré elle d'un principe dont nous aurions été les premiers à enfreindre le maintien.

Dans les deux suppositions que je viens d'analyser, nous

ne saurions nous dissimuler que le résultat serait également défavorable pour nous ; car pour résumer le tout en deux mots, nous aurions à attendre de la Porte : soit *un refus,* compromettant pour notre dignité, soit une *concession* qui aurait pour conséquence immédiate l'entrée d'une escadre anglaise et française dans la mer Noire.

L'un et l'autre de ces résultats sont si graves qu'avant de se décider à en courir la chance, l'intérêt du service de Votre Majesté exige d'examiner sérieusement les conséquences auxquelles nous devrons être preparés ; les sacrifices que la Russie devra faire ; les mesures de prévoyance que nous soyons en état quel que soit l'évènement, de venir à l'appui de la dignité de la Russie si elle est compromise, à la défense de sa sûreté, si elle risque d'être menacée !

En soumettant ces réflexions à Votre Majesté, il en est encore une que j'ose émettre finalement ici, dans l'espoir qu'en l'énonçant je ne saurais manquer, Sire, de rencontrer Votre approbation. Je pense nommément : que le système de politique loyale et généreuse que Votre Majesté a adopté envers le Sultan, conseille au Cabinet Impérial de ne pas placer ce Souverain, notre Allié, dans la pénible nécessité de nous faire une concession, qui l'entraînerait inévitablement dans une complication dangereuse. En effet, la Turquie dans son état de faiblesse et de décadence actuelle, a un égal besoin de pouvoir compter sur la protection de la Russie et de ménager en même tems la susceptibilité des Puissances maritimes. Contraindre la Porte à sortir de cette position, c'est causer sa ruine. Admettons que le Sultan, en nous ouvrant les Dardanelles, veuille les fermer aux anglais et aux français, nous attirons sur la Turquie un danger imminent et nous imposons à nous même l'obligation absolue de venir à son secours ; conséquemment nous acceptons les chances d'une guerre, la plus défavorable de toutes ; d'une guerre où nous n'avons rien à gagner et de grands intérêts commerciaux à perdre. Admettons, au contraire, que le Sultan, cédant aux Puissances maritimes, leur ouvre le passage, nous détruisons de nos propres mains la barrière qui ferait notre sûreté; nous perdons un allié jusqu'ici fidèle, et nous livrons la Turquie à l'influence de l'Angleterre et de la France; en un mot nous risquons de compromettre en un seul jour les résultats que la politique persévérante et la générosité de Votre Majesté ont obtenus durant sept ans, depuis la paix d'Andrinople, jusqu'à la signature de la transaction mémorable conclue par le Cte. Orloff, en dépit de l'Angleterre et de la France à la gloire de la Russie.

Consolider l'œuvre de conservation et de paix que nous devons à la modération de Votre Majesté; assurer le repos de la Russie en éloignant tout ce qui peut troubler la Turquie dans son existence actuelle; maintenir enfin au lieu de l'ébranler, cette barrière politique et morale que les Dardanelles établissent entre nous et les Puissances maritimes dans l'Orient, telle me paraît être l'expression fidèle de la pensée et des volontés de Votre Majesté; tels me semblent aussi les vrais besoins et les intérêts réels de la Russie.

12 janvier 1838 (o.s.).

Menshikov to Nesselrode, *ibid.* 18 janvier 1838.

Je Vous suis bien reconnaissant pour la communication de cette pièce modèle de logique et forte de vérité.

Appendix B

RUSSIA AND ENGLAND

[Pozzo di Borgo to Nesselrode, 21 June/3 July 1838, received at Toeplitz, No. 54, réservée, London, folio 129, R. A.]

[Extract] We must think of our position in case the Pasha declares his independence; at present the Cabinets talk of the Porte and the Pasha, but then he will drop into the background, and Russia will be the theme. Ever since the Restoration England has tried to exert a preponderant influence on France; Wellington supported Polignac because the latter was opposed to Russia; since the July Revolution England has tried to use France for purposes of revolutionary propaganda; Louis Philippe resists this tendency, but an Anglo-French agreement against Russia is to be reckoned with.

[Text] L'Autriche a multiplié ses rapports et resserré ses liens avec nous depuis la révolution de juillet. Le danger qui menaçait son existence a influé sur sa politique, et comme nous avons des intérêts conformes et réciproques à conserver, nous nous sommes entendus afin de remplir un but commun.

Nonobstant les traditions qui peuvent se continuer dans le Cabinet Autrichien sur la nécessité de conserver l'Empire Ottoman, il est naturel que ces maximes se modifient lorsque des circonstances inévitables et qui ne proviennent nullement de la faute ou de l'ambition de la Russie exigeront d'examiner la question sur le terrain où ces circonstances et les évènements l'auront placée; on doit donc s'attendre que si Méhémet Ali se déclare indépendant en dépit de tous les souverains qui auront travaillé à l'en empêcher, la Cour de Vienne fixera son attention sur la position nouvelle du Sultan et sur celle que se sera donnée le sujet rebelle devenu souverain.

Le Sultan verra s'élever contre lui une Puissance formée par la révolte et couronnée par la victoire. Cette Puissance aura plus de ressources physiques et morales et sera la maîtresse de le détruire à volonté.

Dès que ce fait sera constaté, il agira sur la politique de la France et de l'Angleterre qui après avoir dissuadé de bonne foi le Pacha de la prétention de la Souveraineté se disputeront peut-être son amitié en regardant cette souveraineté comme établie.

Sans enumérer les démonstrations qui prouveraient de la manière la plus convaincante que le Sultan aura cessé de régner du moment que Méhémet Ali se déclare indépendant, la prudence demande, surtout de notre part, de regarder cette vérité comme constante.

Malgré une telle conviction, la sagesse de l'Empereur me semble devoir la dissimuler dans les premières mesures que les évènements commanderont de prendre, et cette réserve ne sera nullement un manque de foi, mais une précaution à l'égard des nécessités dans lesquelles la politique de la Russie peut se trouver, malgré toute la bonne foi possible, par le changement de rapports qui peut résulter à la suite de l'indépendance du Pacha.

Pour entrer plus directement en matière, supposons que Méhémet Ali se déclare Souverain. Le Sultan ne peut le reconnaître sans prononcer sa propre déchéance. Alors la guerre éclatera entre lui et son rebelle.

Cette guerre présente peu de chances au premier, et la Russie, restant neutre, risquerait de voir réaliser dans cette occasion ce qu'Ibrahim Pacha aurait exécuté infailliblement, il y a quelques années, lorsqu'il ne lui fallait que faire quelques marches faciles pour s'emparer de Constantinople sans résistance.

Dans la position où il va se trouver, le Sultan doit demander le secours de la Russie qui lui est assuré par le traité.   Cette marche est la plus régulière, et l'Empereur interviendra comme allié et protecteur.

Il est cependant une précaution de plus indispensable à notre sûreté qu'il sera nécessaire de prendre et qui seule peut assurer notre opération immédiate et nos intérêts futurs, savoir: l'augmentation de ce secours au point de mettre la Russie à l'abri des défections des Turcs et des attaques de l'Angleterre et de la France, que nous devons supposer, tout en ne négligeant rien afin de les éviter et de les conjurer s'il est possible.

Dès qu'un seul bataillon Russe entrera dans le Bosphore, les mots: de Constantinople, de Dardanelles, des Indes, d'ambition de la Russie, feront un bruit de tonnerre à Londres et à Paris.   Si donc une démonstration insuffisante exciterait contre nous tous les obstacles que la jalousie peut nous opposer, la prudence et notre salut nous commanderont de convertir cette démonstration en une occupation solide et capable de repousser les attaques de nos ennemis.

Dèsque les armées de l'Empereur seraient établies sur les rives du Bosphore et qu'elles tiendraient les Dardanelles de manière à ne pas craindre d'en être délogées, la Russie peut attendre sans d'autres mouvements excentriques ce qui arrivera ailleurs.

La Mer Noire lui appartient alors sans disputes et toutes les ressources de l'Empire peuvent s'écouler commodément par les voies maritimes et être fournies aux troupes chargées de défendre les points définis et décisifs.

Nous n'irons pas nous éloigner des rives du Bosphore et des Dardanelles pour faire la guerre à Méhémet Ali en Syrie et encore moins en Egypte.   Ce serait une générosité mal conçue que celle de reconquérir à nos dépens les provinces insurgées pour les soumettre au Sultan qui deviendrait notre ennemi du moment où il cessera de nous craindre.

Dans cette grande convulsion il faut s'attendre que ce qui restera de parties éparses de l'Empire du Sultan sera agité par des commotions intérieures, même en sup-

posant que ce Prince existe sous l'égide de la Russie.
Dans ce cas, notre politique, Monsieur le Comte, me semble
devoir nous porter à ne pas y prendre une part active et
matérielle et à ne pas affaiblir notre position principale
pour ce qui se passe sur des points séparés.

Dèsque l'Angleterre et la France seraient convaincues
qu'elles ne pourraient pas nous chasser de cette position
principale, alors les jalousies éclateront entr'elles. La
dernière ne voudra pas se mettre au service de l'autre sans
faire des conquêtes pour son profit et celle-ci craindra
toujours de la voir s'établir utilement dans la Mediterranée
et s'approcher de l'Égypte.

L'infinité, la variété des incidents et des chances qui
se présenteront dans cette guerre sans but défini pour elles,
si ce n'est la jalousie de voir la Russie maîtresse des détroits,
sont incalculables. La Russie, forte dans le poste qu'elle
aura pris, règlera sa politique selon les circonstances et
ne manquera pas de chances utiles. Son attitude, quoique
limitée à ce qui lui convient le plus, sera également plus
imposante, si on la croit inébranlable, et plus respectée
parcequ'elle sera à la fois forte et prudente.

La crise que la dissolution de l'Empire Ottoman amènera
tiendra l'Europe en agitation et en partie en guerre pendant
un temps qu'il est impossible de déterminer d'avance.
Tout commande d'écarter une si terrible épreuve. Si les
Puissances maritimes sont décidées d'y parvenir et de
bonne foi, elles ont des chances probables d'obtenir un but
qui serait évidemment à préférer ; mais si la force et la
nature des évènements rendent cette crise inévitable, la
Russie est appelée à la subir sans surprise et avec des
précautions prises d'avance.

Ses ennemis tenteront de lui susciter des troubles in-
térieurs ; c'est contre de telles éventualités que l'on doit
se prémunir en appliquant toutes ses ressources à la défense de ses propres intérêts.

L'Autriche ne saurait commettre la faute qui lui serait
fatale en adoptant un système opposé. Dèsque l'Empire

Turc est destiné à se dissoudre, sa politique doit la porter à se ménager l'occasion de faire quelques acquisitions utiles et à maintenir son alliance avec la Russie. La sagesse de l'Empereur amènera cette entente aujourd'hui que les Souverains et les Cabinets sont réunis.

La Prusse pensera à la défense de son territoire et de celui de la Confédération. Il n'est pas à présumer que la France, si elle se précipite dans une guerre contre nous, veuille en déclarer une sur ses frontières.

Si ces combinaisons qui semblent si praticables se réalisent, alors la Russie n'aura qu'à défendre et maintenir la position qu'elle aura prise pour assurer la communication des deux mers. Elle verra les évènements se développer et agira en conséquence.

En considérant que le Cabinet Impérial porte une attention si éclairée et constante sur les affaires d'Orient, j'aurais dû m'abstenir de lui soumettre les observations contenues dans la présente dépêche; mais dèsqu'elles se sont présentées à mon esprit, j'ai jugé de mon devoir de lui en offrir le tribut, encouragé par l'indulgence avec laquelle mon zèle a été excusé dans tant d'autres occasions et que j'ai besoin d'implorer encore plus instamment dans celle-ci.

Pozzo di Borgo.

Appendix C

[R. A., Butenev to Nesselrode, No. 17, très réservée, 1/23 October 1838, Constantinople, folio 50.]

[Extract] Public curiosity about Reshid's mission in connection with the treaty of commerce of August 16 and the joint cruise of the British and Turkish fleets.

[Text] À la vérité le négociateur ottoman dans ses explications avec quelquesuns des représentants étrangers et avec notre chargé d'affaires avait lui-même parlé de sa mission dans le même sens que s'en sont exprimés envers moi les ministres turcs dès nos premières entrevues; savoir: qu'elle n'avait d'autre but que de convaincre l'Europe et surtout les Puissances maritimes que la position de la Porte vis-à-vis du Pacha d'Égypte lui devenait plus intolérable de jour en jour et que le maintien du *status quo* minait trop les ressources et menaçait trop la sécurité de l'Empire Ottoman pourque le Sultan ne sentît l'urgente nécessité de voir mettre un terme à cet état de choses par le concours efficace des grandes Puissances. Toutefois cette explication ostensible n'était généralement regardée que comme un voile destiné à couvrir de tout autres plans et combinaisons. Les uns et les plus modérés voyaient dans l'envoi de Réchid Pacha sous de pareils auspices le signal d'un changement du système politique suivi depuis quelques années par la Porte et partant de là un relâchement de son alliance avec la Russie et son rapprochement de plus en plus intime avec l'Angleterre par l'espoir de voir le Gouvernement Britannique prendre fait et cause contre Méhémet Ali. Peut-être cette manière de voir était-elle assez rapprochée de celle de l'Ambassadeur de France lui-même qui semblait avoir conçu de l'ombrage et se montrait blessée de la marche isolée et précipitée de son collègue Britannique. Selon d'autres, qui allaient beaucoup plus loin dans leurs conjonctures, le rapprochement de la Porte avec l'Angleterre était un fait consommé en principe et Réchid Pacha, instrument et complice des vues de Lord Ponsonby, ne s'était chargé de rien moins que de travailler à miner le Traité d'Alliance avec la Russie et de négocier à Londre une alliance non seulement contre le Pacha d'Égypte, mais aussi contre la Perse dans le but éventuel de fair agir d'un côté des forces maritimes formidables contre Alexandrie et la Syrie et de faire entrer de l'autre une Escadre anglaise dans la Mer Noire, destinée à porter des troupes et des munitions pour appuyer les opérations de la Porte contre la Perse. Enfin on allait jusqu'à prétendre que Réchid Pacha n'avait eu l'ordre de passer par Vienne et Berlin que pour s'efforcer d'attirer l'Autriche et la Prusse dans la vaste coalition préparée par l'Angleterre à la fois pour délivrer la Porte de son dangereux vassal et pour soustraire l'Orient à l'influence de la Russie.

Ces suppositions évidemment hasardées et extravagantes ont néanmoins été accréditées ici pendant quelque temps, soit par la crédulité soit par la malveillance et ce qui est hors de doute c'est que l'Ambassade anglaise n'a rien épargné et n'épargne rien jusqu'à présent pour faire croire à l'explosion imminente d'une guerre générale en Orient, dirigée contre la prétendue politique envahissante de la Russie ou plutôt contre son ascendant et sa puissance réelle dans cette partie du monde.

Sans ajouter trop de foi et trop d'importance à ces conjectures et à ces rumeurs exagérées je me suis attaché à observer les faits sans préoccupation et avec calme et à sonder les dispositions des Ministres Turcs placés aujourd' hui à la tête des affaires. Je n'ai pu me dissimuler, il est vrai, l'apparence de réserve que j'ai cru d'abord remarquer dans le langage du Sultan et dans mes premiers entretiens avec ses conseillers et je l'ai signalée dans mes rapports au Ministère Impérial. Je n'ai pu méconnaître également

une augmentation ostensible de l'influence dont l'Ambassadeur d'Angleterre cherche à faire parade ici et dont les
résultats patents sont les uns avantageux aux intérêts
de son Gouvernement, tel qu'un traité de commerce
évidemment onéreux pour la Turquie, les autres constituent
plutôt de puérils succès d'amour-propre, tels que la recon-
naissance de la Belgique et de l'Espagne. Mais j'avoue
qu'à côté de ces efforts et de ces tentatives que fait l'Angleterre pour paraître braver et miner l'influence de la Russie
à Constantinople, je n'ai pas acquis jusqu'à ce moment
la conviction que ces tentatives malveillantes et ces vues
hostiles aient produit une altération véritable dans le
système politique de la Porte et encore moins dans les
dispositions personnelles du Sultan à notre égard. Sans
parler de la démonstration assez remarquable par laquelle ce
Souverain a voulu me donner la mesure du prix qu'il met
à voir une confiance intime présider à ses relations avec la
Russie, ainsi que de sa ferme détermination à repousser
toute déviation de l'esprit et du but du Traité d'alliance
de 1833, je crois même pouvoir avancer que le crédit de
Réchid Pacha, l'auteur et le plus zélé promoteur du rapprochement avec l'Angleterre, paraît baisser à mesure
qu'il s'achémine vers le terme de sa Mission, présumée si
importante et si mystérieuse.

On pourrait dire même que ce crédit n'a jamais été aussi
puissant sur l'esprit du Sultan que le proclament les partisans de l'Angleterre et que s'en flatte Lord Ponsonby tout
le premier. Le conseiller aujourd'hui le plus influent du
Sultan, Mustapha Bey, n'hésite guère à dénigrer le caractère et les vues de Réchid et à regarder d'avance comme
nuls les résultats de sa Mission à Londres; Nouri-Effendi
commence plus timidement à s'exprimer dans le même sens
et quant au vieux Hosrew il porte à Réchid une inimitié
que partage à un bien plus haut degré encore Halil Pacha
qui quoiqu'écarté des affaires en ce moment, nourrit presqu'
aussi évidemment l'espoir de rentrer en grace auprès du
Souverain son Auguste beau-père que celui de pouvoir se

venger du principal auteur de sa chute. A en croire
l'opinion de ces divers personnages, Réchid Pacha en y
arrivant l'année dernière immédiatement après la catas-
trophe de son ancien patron Perteff n'a réussi d'abord à
se soutenir qu'en se montrant adroitement utile et actif
dans les innovations administratives du Sultan dont il sut
embrasser les vues et en faciliter la mise en exécution par
l'application des idées et des notions qu'il avait rapportées
de son séjour en Europe. C'est lui qui mit la dernière
main à l'organisation des nouveaux conseils introduits
aujourd'hui dans le Gouvernement et dont l'action confuse
et incohérente encore sert plutôt à ralentir et à embarrasser
qu'à régulariser la marche des affaires.

La position et le crédit de Réchid Pacha commençait à
peine à se consolider par ces moyens, lorsque l'annonce
des projets d'indépendance du Pacha d'Égypte vint
promptement détourner le Sultan de ses réformes administratives en absorbant toute son attention et en concentrant
toutes ses pensées dans une seule, qui est son idée fixe, celle
de se voir débarrassé de son formidable vassal. L'accord
frappant qui se manifesta alors entre toutes les Puissances
pour s'opposer à l'indépendance de Méhémet Ali ne
suffisait pas augré du Sultan pour sa sécurité et celle de
son Empire; le maintien du *status quo* qui était leur pro-
gramme unanime au lieu de lui paraître une égide protec-
trice lui semblait un obstacle odieux à l'accomplissement
de ses vues. Soit que Réchid Pacha ait prévu que ces
complications extérieures pourraient amener sa disgrâce à
laquelle travaillaient sourdement ses rivaux, soit qu'il fût
déjà rébuté des entraves qu'il rencontrait à chaque pas dans
les projets de réformes et d'innovation qui étaient le principal appui de son crédit auprès du Sultan, soit enfin qu'il
ait réellement entrevu la possibilité de substituer un système
d'alliance avec l'Angleterre à l'alliance de la Russie, ce
Ministre s'attacha dès lors à exploiter l'amour-propre blessé
et l'animosité ardente de Son Souverain contre Méhémet
Ali pour faire entendre que l'Angleterre seule pouvait et

voulait franchement épouser la cause de la Porte contre
le Pacha d'Égypte et que sa puissance et sa situation lui
donnaient les moyens assurés de réduire celui-ci à l'extrémité,
quelques fussent mêmes les dispositions des autres Puissances.

Il paraît que l'Ambassadeur d'Angleterre, qui au premier moment mit de la circonspection dans son langage en
insistant officiellement comme ses collègues sur le maintien
du *status quo* se montra de plus en plus disposé à appuyer
les espérances dont Réchid berçait le Sultan sur l'appui
de l'Angleterre. C'est alors que Lord Ponsonby conclut
avec autant de mystère que de promptitude le fameux traité
de commerce dont une des clauses était l'abolition des
monopoles de l'Égypte, clause qu'il fit envisager à la Porte
comme un lévier décisif dont le Gouvernement Britannique
ne balancerait pas à se servir pour agir ouvertement contre
Méhémet Ali en le contraignant par la force d'exécuter
une condition qui serait l'arrêt de l'anéantissement de ses
richesses et de sa puissance. C'est alors aussi que Lord
Ponsonby proposa en premier lieu la jonction de la flotte
anglaise avec la flotte turque pour une croisière destinée
à imposer au Pacha de l'Égypte et en cas d'aggression de
sa part pour bloquer Alexandrie et agir contre les côtes
de la Syrie et qu'il encouragea hautement l'envoi de Réchid
Pacha à Londres comme le plus sûr moyen d'éclairer l'opinion de l'Europe, de faire envisager sous son vrai jour la
position de la Porte et de déterminer le Gouvernement
Britannique à adopter des mesures décisives, de concert
avec la France son alliée, pour une solution définitive et
satisfaisante de la question d'Égypte. Malgré des insinuations et des promesses faites pour flatter l'idée favorite
du Sultan, Sa Hautesse ne consentit à la jonction des
deux flottes qu'à la suite des déclarations émanées de
l'Empereur Notre Auguste Maître à Toeplitz et qui lui
semblaient de nature à autoriser une telle mesure. Il ne
se décida non plus qu'après quelque hésitation à l'envoi
de Réchid Pacha à Londres en remarquant qu'il était

assez surpris de voir l'Ambassadeur d'Angleterre si prodigue d'espérances et de promesses spontanées aujourd'hui, tandisque quelques années auparavant et au moment des conjonctures les plus critiques de la guerre d'Égypte, la Porte avait vainement sollicité l'assistance du Gouvernement Britannique.   Malgré cette judicieuse réflexion le Sultan dominé par sa haine contre Méhémet Ali se laissa aller à confier à Réchid la mission qu'il convoitait ardemment, en la représentant comme si féconde en résultats avantageux; mais ce qui est assez curieux et remarquable, c'est que dans le Rescrit adressé à cette occasion à la Porte, Sa Hautesse annonce sa détermination d'envoyer Réchid Pacha à Londres dans l'espoir que sa mission atteindrait le but désiré et que dans le cas contraire c'est sur ce ministre seul que retomberait toute la responsabilité du non-succès.   Les Ministres de la Porte furent frappés des termes de ce Rescrit, mais Réchid Pacha ne recula pas et sa précipitation à se mettre en route ainsi que la lenteur qu'il met aujourd'hui à poursuivre son voyage viennent assez à l'appui de l'opinion de ceux qui croient qu'il n'a provoqué lui-même sa mission extraordinaire que pour se mettre honorablement à l'abri d'une disgrâce qu'il appréhendait devoir être prochaine.

Pour résumer en peu de mots les considérations que j'ai pris la liberté d'exposer dans la présente dépêche ainsi . . . je me bornerai à répéter que l'Angleterre et surtout son Ambassadeur à Constantinople n'a rien épargné pour accaparer de l'influence et pour multiplier les occasions de nuire à l'ascendant que la position de la Russie ainsi que la Puissance et la politique magnanime de l'Empereur lui ont acquis dans ce pays-ci à tant de titres.   Mais autant que mes faibles moyens et mon expérience me permettent d'en juger, ces tentatives malveillantes et ces impulsions haineuses n'ont point produit jusqu'ici d'altération sensible dans les dispositions du Sultan ni dans l'esprit de ses conseillers les plus éclairés et les mieux intentionnés.   Je suis donc porté à croire que la crainte salutaire de la puis-

sance se joint au souvenir des services éminents que la
Porte en a reçus pour la faire reculer du moins longtemps
encore à toute idée d'un changement dans la nature des
rapports actuels qui ont valu à la Turquie cinq années de
paix et de tranquillité, de sécurité au dehors et même de
prospérité au dedans, après avoir assuré le salut du trône
ottoman lors dès mémorables évènements de 1833. Ce qui
me paraît encore venir à l'appui de cette manière de voir,
c'est que d'un côté toutes les forces militaires du Sultan et
toutes ses ressources sont concentrées maintenant en Syrie,
sur le point le plus éloigné de nos frontières, ce qui ne prouve
guères d'arrière-pensée de guerre contre la Russie ; et que
de l'autre, quelques soient les tentatives insensées de l'Angleterre pour provoquer une guerre semblable, les Turcs ne
sont pas assez aveugles ou ignorants pour ne pas prévoir
que non seulement Elle ne pourrait songer à avoir l'Autriche
pour alliée contre nous, mais qu'Elle ne peut même dans les
conjonctures du moment compter sur l'alliance de la France
qui est loin de partager ses vues dans la question d'Égypte
et dont l'Ambassadeur n'hésite pas à dénier toute participation aux suggestions passionnées et aux récents actes de son
collègue Britannique. . . .

[received 25 Oct. 1838.]

[Nesselrode to Butenev, 27 October 1838, o.s., No. 1441,
folio 50, Constantinople.]

L'Empereur a fixé son attention sérieuse sur les dépêches
que Vous m'avez adressées depuis Votre retour à Constantinople. Votre présence y était réclamée plus que jamais
dans un moment où l'activité du Gouvernement Anglais
tend indubitablement à miner notre influence conservatrice
en Turquie et à nuire à l'union si heureusement établie entre
notre Cabinet et la Porte Ottomane.

Cette tendance que plus d'un indice nous avait mani-
festée avant votre arrivée à Constantinople nous a été
démontrée depuis par les informations pleines d'intérêt
contenues dans les dernières dépêches de V. Excellence.

Celles du Comte Pozzo di Borgo viennent encore à l'appui de Vos réflexions judicieuses et nous confirment dans l'opinion que partout l'action du Cabinet de Londres se dirige en ce moment contre nous avec un redoublement de jalousie et de malveillance. . . .

[Extract] Constantinople is the danger-point, must stiffen the Sultan. . . . [Text] Notre Auguste Maître croit n'avoir aucun motif fondé de croire que les conseils perfides de Lord Ponsonby ayent agi sur la conviction du Sultan et ébranlé la confiance qu'il place dans la Russie. . . . [Extract] Approves of relations with Mustapha Bey, is pleased by Sultan's assurance [Text] "que jamais sous aucun prétexte il ne consentirait à laisser entrer une escadre anglaise dans les Dardanelles, qu'une pareille demande, si elle venait à être faite de la part de l'Angleterre, serait repoussée comme elle le méritait, enfin que dans le cas où une semblable tentative serait faite par surprise, la Porte ne pourrait y voir qu'une disposition hostile contr'-Elle et se hâterait, le cas échéant, à se concerter avec le Cabinet Impérial sur la marche qu'Elle aurait à suivre."

[Extract] This is convincing. . . . [Text] Mais d'un autre côté nous n'ignorons pas combien la politique du Divan est vacillante et mobile ; combien l'influence étrangère y amène souvent des changements imprévus et rapides. Cette considération nous oblige à employer tous les moyens de surveillance en notre pouvoir afin de pénétrer les desseins des Anglais et de paralyser leur malfaisante activité à Constantinople. . . .

Notre Auguste Maître Vous recommande spécialement de profiter de Vos relations confidentielles avec le dernier [Mustapha Bey] pour appeler l'attention du Sultan sur l'inopportunité de prolonger la réunion de l'Escadre Turque avec les forces navales de l'Angleterre, et nommément sur l'étrange imprévoyance avec laquelle on a admis des officiers Anglais à bord des vaisseaux de guerre ottomans. Ne dissimulez point, Monsieur, la surprise et la désapprobation que ce fait a rencontrés chez nous. Sans montrer à ce

sujet une susceptibilité intempestive il est bon toutefois
de faire sentir aux Ministres turcs que nous tenons nos
regards attentivement fixés sur leur conduite; et que si
d'un côté notre Cabinet est loin de leur susciter la moindre
tracasserie gratuite, il est fermement résolu d'une autre
part à ne passer sous silence aucun incident qui soit de
nature à altérer la bonne intelligence et la confiance mutuelle si heureusement établie entre la Russie et la Porte.
Sous ce rapport il Vous appartient, Monsieur, de signaler
franchement au Sultan l'inconvenant et le danger qu'il y
aurait à prolonger la présence des officiers anglais sur les
vaisseaux turcs ainsi que les conséquences fâcheuses qui
peuvent se rattacher à la jonction des deux Escadres, si
elle devait se prolonger encore plus longtemps. Veuillez
imprimer aux réflexions que Vous adresserez à ce sujet au
confidant de Sa Hautesse ce caractère de bienveillance qui
convient si bien à la politique loyale et désintéressée de
notre Auguste Maître. Mais ne négligez non plus rien de
ce qui peut agir fortement sur l'esprit du Sultan pour le
décider à mettre fin à la réunion des deux escadres; démonstration qui ne produira aucun effet sur le Pacha d'Égypte
contre lequel elle est censée être dirigée tandisqu'elle sert
en réalité à mettre les forces navales de la Turquie à la
merci de la Grande Bretagne. Convient-il aux intérêts
et à la dignite du Sultan de laisser sa flotte entre les mains
des Anglais et de la livrer pour ainsi dire en ôtage à la
politique capricieuse et passionnée de Lord Palmerston?
Voilà la réflexion qui devrait se présenter d'elle-même à
l'esprit de Sa Hautesse et qu'il ne Vous sera pas difficile de
suggérer à son confidant. Une autre question qu'il ne sera
pas inutile non plus de lui adresser sera celle-ci: que dirait
l'Angleterre si l'idée venait à l'Empereur de demander à
Sa Hautesse de mettre des officiers russes à bord des vaisseaux turcs et comment le Sultan refuserait-il à l'Empereur
son Ami et Allié, une demande qui vient d'être accordée à
l'Angleterre? Cette considération acheverait sans doute
de démontrer à la Porte combien il est désirable pour elle

de sortir de l'embarras dans lequel elle s'est placée et de
faire cesser un moment plus tôt l'action simultanée des
deux Escadres. L'approche de la mauvaise saison ne
saurait manquer d'ailleur à fournir au Gouvernement Ottoman un motif plausible pour faire rentrer sa flotte dans le
Bosphore et pour mettre tout simplement un terme à sa
réunion à l'Escadre Anglaise sans que le Gouvernement
Britannique puisse se montrer blessé du rappel des forces
navales du Sultan à une époque où la navigation dans
l'Archipel présente des dangers réels. Il Vous appartient,
Monsieur, de faire valoir ces réflexions et de veiller surtout
à ce qu'à l'époque du retour de l'escadre Turque, les officiers
anglais qui s'y trouvent à bord en soyent éloignés sans éclat
mais de manière à leur enlever à l'avenir toute influence
nuisible sur la marine ottomane. Vos relations personnelles
avec le Capitan Pacha devront Vous faciliter à cet égard
les moyens nécessaires pour remplir les instructions de
l'Empereur dans toute leur étendue.

. . . Quant aux assurances qu'elles [your despatches of
27 Sept/9 Oct] renferment sur l'intention positive du
Sultan de se mettre en garde contre toute tentative que
feraient les Anglais de s'introduire *sous un prétexte quelconque* dans le canal des Dardanelles, Notre Auguste Maître
Vous charge d'en prendre formellement acte en son nom
et de témoigner à Sa Hautesse combien Il Se plaît à
compter sur la fidélité avec laquelle ce Monarque saura
remplir à cet égard ses engagements qui sont d'ailleurs
intimement liés aux intérêts de sa propre sûreté et de la
dignité de la Turquie.

Recevez, etc.

[Nesselrode to Butenev, très secrète, No. 1442, 27 October
1838, o.s., folio 50, Constantinople.]

[Extract] The Anglo-Turk trade treaty is regarded as
very important for England; France looks on it with
jealousy. It must be examined from the *commercial* and
the *political* aspects.

[Text] Quant aux résultats commerciaux qui se rattachent au traité signé par Lord Ponsonby, il se présente à
nos yeux une question qu'il nous importe avant tout de
résoudre, savoir: "quelle est l'influence que cette transaction peut exercer sur *notre propre commerce.*"

Dans un entretien que j'ai eu dernièrement à ce sujet
avec M. le Comte Cancrine, ce Ministre m'a témoigné le
désir de posséder des renseignements détaillés de nature à
éclaircir ses doutes sur la question que je viens de poser.

Je m'empresse d'inviter Votre Excellence à vouloir bien
me mettre à même de communiquer à ce sujet à M. le
Ministre des Finances toutes les informations qui peuvent
lui offrir quelque intérêt. Il vous sera facile, Monsieur, de
les recueillir auprès de ceux de nos négociants qu'un long
séjour en Turquie joint à une expérience pratique des
opérations commerciales dans le Levant autorise à porter
sur cette matière une opinion solide. Ils seront intéressés
les premiers à se rendre compte de l'influence que les facilités accordées aux négociants anglais et l'abolition des
monopoles dans tout l'empire Ottoman peuvent produire
sur nos relations commerciales avec cet Empire. De plus,
habitués comme ils le sont à entretenir des communications
journalières avec nos ports de la Mer Noire ils seront
également en état de Vous fournir des notions dignes de
foi sur les conséquences que la transaction conclue entre
la Porte et l'Angleterre peut avoir sur la prospérité com-
merciale des provinces du Midi de la Russie. Toute con-
jecture à ce sujet serait prématurée tant qu'elle ne serait
pas fondée sur des renseignements positifs et puisés sur
les lieux mêmes.

En admettant que le traité conclu par Lord Ponsonby
ne porte aucun préjudice aux intérêts directs de notre
propre commerce, l'Empereur ne pourrait voir qu'avec
satisfaction les avantages que cette transaction promettrait
au Gouvernement Ottoman, s'il est vrai qu'il lui soit favorable. En ce cas Notre Auguste Maître féliciterait sin-
cèrement le Sultan des résultats avantageux qu'il aurait

obtenus. Mais avant de Vous prononcer dans ce sens envers les Ministres de Sa Hautesse, il sera prudent, Monsieur, de bien approfondir les considérations *politiques* qui se rattachent à la transaction dont il s'agit.

Nul doute que Lord Ponsonby en la signant n'ait eu principalement en vue de faire entrevoir au Sultan que l'abolition des monopoles dans toute l'etendue de son Empire porterait un coup mortel à la puissance du Pacha d'Égypte. Par ce moyen l'Ambassadeur Britannique en flattant les sentiments de vengeance que le Sultan entretient à l'égard de son dangereux vassal a espéré relever l'influence politique de l'Angleterre en Turquie. D'une autre part Lord Ponsonby a pensé aussi qu'il réserverait en même temps à son Gouvernement la faculté d'intervenir dans les affaires d'Égypte, à l'appui des stipulations d'un traité formel dans le cas où Méhémet Ali refuserait d'y souscrire. Or, celui-ci, venant d'y adhérer sans la moindre difficulté, ainsi que les dernières nouvelles d'Alexandrie nous l'annoncent, toute la combinaison de Lord Ponsonby semble tomber d'elle-même. Le Vice-Roi, maître absolu de tous les biens-fonds en Égypte, et par conséquent propriétaire exclusif de ses récoltes, paraît voir avec indifférence l'abolition d'un système de monopole qui ne saurait l'atteindre. En effet il reste comme par le passé l'unique arbitre des produits du sol qu'il possède à lui seul. Le traité de Lord Ponsonby est donc frappé de nullité quant à l'Egypte ; l'espoir de détruire les ressources financières de Méhémet Ali se trouve dèçu ; et la Porte trompée dans son attente finira par se convaincre une fois de plus combien les promesses de l'Angleterre sont illusoires et stériles.

Telle sera, selon toute apparence, l'issue de la combinaison politique dont Lord Ponsonby s'est promis un si grand succès.

Il nous reste à examiner et à savoir si le traité que cet ambassadeur a conclu ne renferme point quelque clause qui nous est encore inconnue, et qui aurait pour objet de neutraliser les relations établies entre nous et la Porte en vertu de notre traité d'alliance.

Voilà le doute que l'Empereur croit doublement nécessaire d'éclaircir dans un moment où nous voyons le Gouvernement Anglais activement employé à nous susciter
partout des embarras et à miner notre influence au dehors.

Notre Auguste Maître Vous charge donc expressément
du soin de sonder attentivement le terrain à Constantinople
afin de constater si les insinuations perfides de l'Ambassadeur Britannique ont réussi à ébranler le système politique
adopté jusqu'ici par le Sultan et si la transaction conclue
par Lord Ponsonby se lie à quelques engagements secrets
contraires à ceux que la Porte a contractés envers nous.

L'Empereur en Vous recommandant le soin d'approfondir à cet égard l'exacte vérité n'ignore combien cette tâche
est délicate et difficile.   Manifester aux Ministres Ottomans la moindre inquiétude ce serait leur donner un signe
de faiblesse qui ne convient point à la position forte et
prépondérante de la Russie.   Les interpeller directement
ce serait manquer indubitablement notre but; car ils
n'hésiteraient point de nier l'existence d'un fait qu'ils
auraient un intérêt réel à nous cacher.   Malgré ces diffi-
cultés dont l'Empereur ne dissimule point la gravité, Sa
Majesté tient à connaître la vérité quelle qu'elle puisse
être.   Elle veut savoir avant tout si la confiance qu'Elle
a placée jusqu'ici dans les intentions du Sultan continue
à être justifiée par la conduite politique de ce Souverain,
ou bien, si un changement survenu dans l'attitude de la
Porte peut nous obliger à notre tour à modifier la nôtre.
Cette question qui se rattache à tout notre système politique
dans l'Orient est trop grave pour qu'elle ne mérite pas de
faire l'object de Vos méditations les plus sérieuses.
Également éloignés d'une inquiétude prématurée comme
d'une sécurité aveugle, nous devons chercher à nous rendre
compte de la situation réelle des choses à Constantinople;
des progrès que l'Angleterre peut y avoir faits dans des
vues qui nous sont contraires; enfin, des conséquences
qu'un pareil changement peut amener dans l'attitude politique de la Porte Ottomane. . . .

[Butenev to Nesselrode, très réservée, 22 November/4 December 1838, folio 50, No. 31, Constantinople, received 7 December, o.s.]

[Extract] Through Mustapha Bey Butenev will transmit to Sultan Emperor's opinions on junction of the two fleets and on treaty of commerce with England and will get assurance that foreign ships of war *under no pretext* will be admitted to the Dardanelles. . . . Will make every effort to find out if the Ponsonby-Reshid commercial treaty contains any secret clauses connected with Reshid's extraordinary mission to London.

[Text] Mais s'il m'est permis en attendant et sans rien préjuger d'énoncer mes conjectures personnelles sur cette question, je serais assez porté à mettre en doute l'existence de clauses secrètes et politiques dans le traité de commerce du 16 août. Les motifs de ma manière de voir à cet égard se fondent en partie sur l'assurance positive et spontanée de la non-existence d'aucune clause secrète qui m'a été donnée par le principal rédacteur de ce traité, M. Bulwer . . . dans une conversation que j'ai eue avec lui avant son départ et dans laquelle il avait mis cette question sur le tapis de son propre mouvement et sans que j'aie cherché à la provoquer. Cette assurance que Mr. Bulwer a également répétée tout aussi spontanément à mes deux collègues d'Autriche et de Prusse venant de la part d'un homme qui s'est généralement concilié ici de l'estime par la modération de son caractère et de ses principes et qui de plus est destiné à aller remplir un emploi marquant à l'Ambassade Britannique à St. Petersbourg me parait constituer une certaine autorité, en pareille matière.

D'un autre côté il m'est revenu d'assez bonne source que l'Ambassadeur de France en se prêtant bien malgré lui à adhérer à un Traité qu'il avait blâmé hautement et auquel il n'a pas dissimulé que son Gouvernement même ne s'était associé qu'avec répugnance avait tâché de sonder le terrain auprès des Turcs pour savoir s'il existait ou non des articles secrets dans le traité en question. Ce n'est qu'après avoir eu lieu de conclure avec quelque vraisemblance qu'il n'en existait point, que cet Ambassadeur paraît n'avoir plus hésité à mettre à exécution les instructions qu'il a reçues de son Gouvernement par rapport à son adhésion au Traité de Commerce du 16 août, dont il vient en effet de signer l'instrument avec les Ministres Ottomans dans une conference *ad hoc* du 13/25 du courant.   J'ai su également que l'Amiral Roussin, apparemment pour ne pas avoir l'air de signer textuellement sans changement ni restriction cette même transaction negociée isolément et à son insu . . . et contre laquelle il s'était lui-même prononcé d'abord, avait insisté sur quelques légères modifications plutôt pour la forme que pour le fond; mais les Ministres Ottomans s'y sont opposés et le traité conclu avec la France se trouve absolument identique à celui de l'Angleterre.

L'Internonce d'Autriche et l'Envoyé de la Prusse ont bien voulu tous deux me donner connaissance confidentiellement des dépêches de Leurs Cours, relatives aux explications que Réchid Pacha a eues avec les deux Cabinets à son passage par Vienne et Berlin.   J'avoue que le langage que M. de Werther announce avoir tenu au négociateur ottoman m'a paru aussi clair que satisfaisant tandisque j'ai eu de la peine à me faire une idée précise de la portée des entretiens de M. le Prince de Metternich avec le Ministre Turc au moins autant que j'ai pu en juger par le résumé de ces entretiens, tel qu'il est rapporté dans les dépêches adressées par le Chancelier de Cour et d'Etat à Mr. le Baron de Stürmer en date du 13 novembre.

[Butenev to Nesselrode, 13/25 December 1838, Constantinople, folio 50, No. 40, received 31 December, o.s.]

[Extract] Confidential notice handed to Mustapha Bey on November 17 o.s.; Sultan's reply received November 29 o.s.   This shows unusual interest of Sultan in these questions.   It has two features:

[Text] En premier lieu Sa Hautesse a l'air de vouloir

se disculper de tout rapprochement suspect avec le Gouvernement Anglais en cherchant à rattacher la mesure de
la jonction de sa flotte avec celle de l'amiral Stopford à
l'effet des déclarations si bienveillantes pour les intérêts
de la Porte émanées de Sa Majesté Impériale à Toeplitz
et en déclarant péremptoirement que dans aucun cas le
Sultan ne souffrirait jamais qu'il soit porté la moindre
atteinte à ses rapports d'amitié intime et d'alliance avec
la Russie, voulant évidemment faire allusion par là aux
tentatives assidues et acharnées de la politique anglaise
pour troubler ces rapports.

En second lieu, le Sultan, en avouant sans déguisement
qu'à ses yeux la question d'Égypte est en ce moment la
plus importante de toutes pour les intérêts politiques de
son trône et de son Empire, semble vouloir se réserver
d'invoquer plus tard le puissant et généreux appui de
l'Empereur, Son Auguste Allié, pour amener cette question
à une solution satisfaisante si la coopération de l'Angleterre, objet présumé des négociations de Réchid Pacha à
Londres, venait à se réduire à de vaines paroles sans effet.

Enfin, quant à l'article des officiers instructeurs anglais,
la communication Turque affirme qu'il n'y en a que deux
seulement qui s'étant montrés particulièrement zélés et
utiles par leurs connaissances techniques, au Capitan Pasha,
durant la croisière combinée des deux Escadres, ont reçu
la proposition d'être attachés pour quelque temps à
l'amirauté turque et se sont d'abord rendus en Angleterre
pour en demander l'autorisation de leur Gouvernement.
. . . [Extract] This is all right if the number and political importance of the instructors is limited. . . .
[Text] Mais j'ai pénétré dans le cours de mes explications
confidentielles à ce sujet que la question de l'admission
d'un nombre considérable d'officiers de marine anglais au
service de la Porte avait été mise sur le tapis avant le
départ de Réchid Pacha pour Londres et chaudement
appuyée par ce Ministre, au fort de son engouement pour
les suggestions de Lord Ponsonby et de ses prédilections

pour l'Angleterre dont il cherchait à se concilier les bonnes grâces et à faire espérer au Sultan·la coopération efficace dans l'affaire d'Égypte. Il paraît que ce fut alors même que des ordres secrets furent adressés à l'Ambassadeur Ottoman à Londres, Fethi Pacha, pour choisir et envoyer ici des officiers instructeurs pour la marine. Mais avec la lenteur ordinaire qui caractérise les Turcs, cette commission avait essuyé des retards.

Aujourd'hui les Ministres Ottomans, en me communiquant ou plutôt en me faisant entendre confidentiellement ces antécédents et en rejetant la responsabilité du fait sur Fethi Pacha et sur Réchid Pacha, m'ont donné l'assurance qu'après plus mure réflexion la Porte avait déjà envoyé depuis quelque temps des contr'ordres à l'Ambassadeur Extraordinaire du Sultan à Londres pour révoquer formellement l'admission d'un certain nombre d'officiers anglais hormis les deux seuls individus demandés spécialement. . . . Les Ministres ajoutèrent que si même par l'effet de quelque contretemps ou malentendus les divers officiers et instructeurs que Fethi Achmet Pacha avait été précédemment chargé d'engager venaient à arriver à Constantinople, la Porte ne balancerait pas à décliner leurs services. J'ai tout lieu d'être convaincu que non seulement cette déclaration des Ministres Ottomans à laquelle j'aurai soin de me référer en temps et lieu a été provoquée par les observations sérieuses exposées au nom de la Cour Impériale dans ma notice soumise au Sultan mais même que ce n'est qu'à la suite de cette démarche de ma part et non pas de propos déliberé et antérieurement que la Porte s'est décidée d'envoyer contr'ordre à Réchid Pacha à Londres pour révoquer la mesure si imprudemment suggérée par ce même Ministre lui-même.

Il faut espérer que ce négociateur, en recevant dans cette occasion un nouvel avertissement qui lui donne la mesure de l'attention et des égards que Son Gouvernement accorde aux conseils de la Russie, se montrera plus circonspect dans sa conduite et dans son aveugle déférence pour le Cabinet

Anglais. Mais si au contraire Réchid Pacha poursuivant
le rôle qu'il a joué ici et dans le but de donner de l'importance à sa mission en même temps que pour maintenir son
crédit chancelant auprès de Son Maître s'efforce d'entretenir le Sultan dans l'espoir d'une coopération prochaine
et efficace de l'Angleterre dans l'affaire d'Égypte, nous
devrons alors nous attendre à de nouveaux conflits d'influence ici. Et si à son tour Lord Palmerston dans la vue
de gagner du temps se montrait disposé à flatter par des
promesses ou par des démonstrations plus ou moins
sérieuses les velléités belliqueuses du Sultan contre le
Pacha d'Égypte, je ne serais pas étonné que Réchid Pacha
n'essayât encore une fois, secondé comme il le sera sans
doute ici par les impulsions passionnées de Lord Ponsonby,
d'entraîner le Souverain Ottoman à quelque démarche
fausse et gratuite comme l'a été la jonction des deux
escadres Turque et Anglaise, peut-être même de lui suggérer quelque résolution brusque et précipitée comme par
exemple une levée de boucliers contre Ibrahim Pacha en
Syrie, s'il y est encouragé par des promesses d'une coopération navale par l'Angleterre.

Mes appréhensions sous ce rapport s'accordent jusqu'à
un certain point avec celles que nourrit de son côté. . . .
Medem, sur quelque nouvelle explosion de l'ambition im-
patiente et mal contenue du Pacha d'Égypte, à l'époque
du printemps. On ne saurait se dissimuler que de part et
d'autre le feu couve sous la cendre et que l'animosité et le
ressentiment du Sultan contre son vassal ne font que
s'accroître. La politique anglaise ne se lasse jamais d'exploiter ces dispositions, au profit de ses vues et de ses
intérêts et d'un autre côté la Porte ne cesse depuis 6 mois
de diriger des renforts de troupes et des envois de munitions
de toute espèce à l'armée du Taurus commandée par Hafiz
Pacha. Ce dernier paraît lui-même assez présumer de la
force et du bon état de son armée, de ses propres talents
militaires et des dispositions favorables manifestées pour
la cause du Sultan par les populations de la Syrie pour

alimenter plus que la prudence et l'expérience du passé ne
devraient le comporter les velléités bien connues de son
Souverain et sa haine contre Méhémet Ali. Cette haine
aveugle et passionnée est aussi le lévier que la politique
de l'Angleterre emploie constamment avec plus ou moins
de succès pour tenter de relâcher l'alliance du Sultan avec
la Russie, tantôt en insinuant que nous soutenons secrète-
ment le Pacha d'Égypte par nos conseils, tantôt que nous
lui fournissons des subsides. Ces tentatives et ces insinuations malveillantes n'obtiennent pas sans doute tout l'effet
désiré, mais elles tiennent le Sultan en haleine et donnent
quelque prise à la politique inquiète et hostile de l'Angleterre. Je persiste à douter toutefois que ces menées aient
abouti à quelques stipulations secrètes dans le traité de
commerce conclu par Lord Ponsonby, autant que j'en puis
juger du moins par toutes les investigations faites
jusqu'ici et que je continuerai avec persévérance. . . .

INDEX

INDEX